the
natural knitter

the natural knitter

How to Choose, Use, and Knit Natural Fibers from Alpaca to Yak

BY BARBARA ALBRIGHT

PHOTOGRAPHS BY ALEXANDRA GRABLEWSKI

POTTER
CRAFT

New York

Published in the United States by Potter Craft,
an imprint of the Crown Publishing Group,
a division of Random House, Inc., New York.

www.crownpublishing.com
www.clarksonpotter.com
www.pottercraftnews.com

POTTER CRAFT and CLARKSON N. POTTER
are trademarks, and POTTER and colophon
are registered trademarks of Random House, Inc.

Library of Congress Cataloging-in-Publication Data
Albright, Barbara.
The natural knitter : how to choose, use, and knit natural fibers from alpaca
to yak / Barbara Albright ; photographs by Alexandra Grablewski.
      p. cm.
   Includes index.
1. Knitting 2. Yarn. I. Title.
   TT820.A42   2006
   746.43'2—dc22

ISBN-13: 978-1-4000-5352-0
ISBN-10: 1-4000-5352-8

Printed in China

DESIGN BY Chalkley Calderwood Pratt

PHOTOGRAPHY BY Alexandra Grablewski

10 9 8 7 6 5 4 3 2 1

First Edition

WHAT HAS BEEN MY "DREAM BOOK," I DEDICATE TO MY CHILDREN, SAMANTHA AND STONE.

ALWAYS BELIEVE IN THE BEAUTY OF YOUR DREAMS, THE POSSIBILITES ARE ENDLESS.

AND MAY YOUR DREAMS BE AS SWEET AND TRUE AS MINE.

I LOVE YOU BOTH VERY MUCH.

Contents

INTRODUCTION

There is nothing like having a wad of cashmere fiber or yarn in your pocket. If you walk into a room full of knitters, pull it out, and casually mention what you are holding, it is as if you were the candy man or a drug dealer holding a contraband item—all the knitters will stop what they are doing and feel the fiber! Most fiber aficionados will immediately put down their knitting so they can touch, stroke, and fondle the yarn. If you have somehow gotten your hands on some incredibly pricey and rare ultrafine vicuna, you will probably hear dumbfounded silence from those who know what a treasure you have.

This is the way we devoted knitters are. For instance, my eyes glaze over if I hear talk of golf, hunting, or fishing.

However, if the subject switches to fiber or knitting, or food, I am all ears and ready to join the party!

Why does knitting elicit such a crazed passion? There is something natural and centering about using two thin sticks to turn string into something useful to wear, give as a gift, keep you warm, or decorate your home. The rhythmic making of one stitch . . . then another . . . then another is calming and therapeutic. Plus, knitting is satisfying because you can make items that are exactly as you want them to be.

Fibers are at the core of knitting, and there is a wide range of wonderful natural yarns that are available and becoming more accessible as knitters

seek the creature comforts that only Mother Nature can offer. *The Natural Knitter* is devoted *entirely* to these luxurious, wonderful natural fibers that set all knitters' hearts fluttering, and tells you everything you need to know about knitting with them. It begins with wool, because wool is the wonder fiber that goes on and on and has memory to beat the band compared to some of the other glorious animal fibers, including alpaca, cashmere, llama, and mohair. Plus, it's readily available and inexpensive. Also not to be missed are the many natural plant fibers, such as cotton, linen, and hemp. This book has them all.

The Natural Knitter also features patterns from some of the world's most talented knitting designers.

In addition to writing about knitting, I also frequently write about organic food and

Opposite and below, from left to right
Tagged sheep, like the one pictured, can be found at the sheep and wool festivals that take place at county fairgrounds all across America. A bucket of Cotswold wool awaits a Rapunzel to spin and dye it into a lustrous yarn with rich, deep colors. Spinning wheels come in many different sizes and styles, but all require steady hands. Whether handspun or not, lofty balls of angora yarn can be yours to keep long after the fiber festivals have packed up their tents.

Many knitters are discovering that the next visit on the fiber trail is spinning their own yarn, bringing them just one step closer to all-natural knitting.

Not only does wool make a superb yarn on its own, it is also the perfect partner to blend with other less bouncy fibers, and to fibers that lack elasticity.

fiber has different characteristics. However, the one quality that all wool has in common is its resiliency and "memory." Not only does wool make a superb yarn on its own, it is also the perfect partner to blend with other less bouncy fibers, and to fibers that lack elasticity.

In addition to sheep, there are many other animals that produce wonderful luxury fibers, among them llamas, alpacas, cashmere and angora goats (mohair comes from the latter), and fluffy angora bunnies. Beyond some of the more recognizable fiber-producing creatures, intriguing fibers can come from other animals as well, including your dog or cat, a buffalo, or even the silver fox that lurks in the woods. These and other fiber-bearing animals are the focus of chapter two.

Chapter two also takes an in-depth look at sumptuous silk. In terms of luxury, silk is in a league of its own. Coming from the cocoon of the silkworm, it can either be unwound and spun from the cocoon while the worm is still inside, or it can be spun from the cocoon after the moth has emerged. Silk's unique structure as an animal protein fiber, derived from extruded filaments, endows it with qualities unmatched by other fibers—animal or plant.

Chapter three turns your attention to the world of plants, which also provide some wonderful fibers—from cotton to linen to the bast fibers. You might be surprised to learn that cotton grows in a variety of colors. While it is illegal to grow hemp in the United States, it is a very environmentally friendly fiber. We get linen (which can last for hundreds of years) from flax and ramie from the genus *Boehmeria*, belonging to the nettle family; and even pineapple is a source of fiber (and I don't mean just the dietary variety!).

sustainable agriculture (farming in an earth-friendly manner). While I was writing an article on organic yarn for *Vogue Knitting*, I became absolutely enchanted with what I was learning about the fibers and the people who bring them to us. These dedicated people made a commitment to be as true to the planet as they could be and were raising fiber according to their demanding standards. This book also salutes some of the committed and pioneering entrepreneurs responsible for making these fibers for knitters. (Of course, the animals and plants that give us these fibers play a *very* important role as well.)

About *The Natural Knitter*

This book is organized into chapters, with chapter one being devoted to wool, because it is the most versatile of yarns available to knitters. There are many different breeds of sheep, each of whose

In chapter four you will discover that there are many plants that can be used to dye yarns in an array of wonderful and beautiful colors. The chapter includes some projects that are knit with plant-dyed yarns as well as information on entrepreneurs who are creating beautiful plant-dyed yarns. For the adventurous, there are step-by-step instructions on how to do a little natural dyeing of your own.

And this leads us to natural next steps, which are the focus of the last chapter. Here you will learn what goes into making a yarn as well as some basic instructions for learning how to spin. There is also a felted and beaded project that is made with wool before it is spun into yarn.

Of course, to accommodate this passion for all things knitted and natural, the natural knitter needs some natural accessories. Happily, there are artisans making beautiful accessories to add to the pleasure of knitting with natural fibers. You will find information on them in the resources.

THE LEVELS OF "NATURALNESS"

All of the projects in this book have been made with natural fibers, whether from a plant or an animal. In some cases, these fibers have been shorn from the animals; in other cases, they have been brushed out of the fur; sometimes the fiber has been collected after it was shed. Plants were picked, then processed for their fiber. Some of the natural fibers are both organic and naturally colored; others are dyed with plant dyes (which may or may not be organic), while some natural fibers are processed by larger yarn companies and dyed with a commercial dye.

All these yarns have a place in a knitter's life, so don't get too carried away about which yarn is the *most* natural. Armed with the information you glean from this book, you will have a greater understanding and a new appreciation of the wide variety of natural yarns that are available. With information on the specialty yarns, you will also be able to choose the correct yarn that is a perfect fit for your special project.

What Makes Yarn Organic?

While this book is about natural fibers, it is also about people who take another step toward being more earth-friendly and create organic yarns. My research into this fairly new segment of the booming organic industry has revealed that the people producing organic yarn and fibers are committed to farming in harmony with the earth. They are all doing the best they can to invent more effective techniques to produce organic fiber and work in a manner that is environmentally friendly.

WHAT DOES "ORGANIC" MEAN EXACTLY?

In the past, organic food and fiber producers established regional voluntary certification programs to define *organic*. Organic farmers and producers have worked together to be more precise about the meaning of the term.

USDA Standards for Producing Organic Animal or Plant Fibers

In a nutshell, a fiber or yarn can qualify as organic only if the following standards are adhered to in its production:

GRAZING AND FEED	MEDICATIONS	CHEMICALS	PESTICIDES/ FERTILIZERS	WASHING	SPINNING	HANDLING
The fiber-producing animal can graze only on organic pastures in the summer and must be fed primarily organic natural, nongenetically modified feeds in the winter.	The animal cannot receive routine antibiotics, wormers, or other medications.	No chemicals can be applied topically to control parasites on the animal.	Fiber plants (such as cotton) must be grown without the use of synthetic pesticides and fertilizers.	The fiber (animal or plant) has to be washed/scoured without the use of chemicals or bleach. Additionally, it cannot be chemically treated with moth-proofing or flame-retardant finishes.	The yarn must be spun using organic spinning oils and with no petroleum-based oils.	Organic fibers must be handled separately from conventionally produced fibers to avoid contamination.

The United States Department of Agriculture (USDA) has in place a set of national standards that strictly define the term *organic*. While their major purpose right now is to define organic foods, the national standards apply to the production of animals and plants that are used as a source of fiber as well. The federal regulations provide precise definitions. Because of them, now we can be assured that not only will the foods we buy be truly organic, but so will our fibers, yarns, and clothes! In addition, the Organic Trade Association (OTA), a membership-based business association, is continuing to work on establishing standards for processing after the fiber has been raised (such as washing the fleeces and spinning the wool).

These are the basics of organic fiber production. It is an ever-evolving and growing part of agricul-ture. Due to increasing demand, more organic yarns are becoming available. Keep your eyes and ears open for people who are farming in a sustainable manner near where you live or when you travel. When you become acquainted with the organic farmers and ranchers, you will come to understand what they are all about and why they have chosen to farm in an environmentally friendly manner. You will probably find that they not only want to do something good for the earth, but they also want to avoid handling chemicals or raising their families near possible toxins.

Go to farmers' markets or fiber festivals and talk to the shepherds. Getting to know the producers of your fiber will help you get back in touch with the earth. (And buying local also cuts down on the amount of fuel needed to transport the fiber.)

Why Buy Organic?

There are several reasons to knit with organic yarn.

By purchasing organic fiber, you are supporting a system of agriculture that works to build healthy soils and a healthy environment. This type of agricultural system does not use toxic inputs that can result in the contamination of the earth, air, and water through the use of toxic pesticides and fertilizers. It is a choice that nurtures nature and celebrates the naturally good things in life.

For people with multiple chemical sensitivities, organic fibers are a great choice. Think about it: some people say they are allergic to wool, but is it the wool or is it the sprays with which the animal was treated or the chemicals in the soaps or oils with which the wool was processed? Or is it an allergy to a chemical dye or a moth-proofing finish? The structure of the wool's fiber is very porous and you can never wash out everything that has come into contact with it.

Organic yarn also just looks and feels great!

How organic is your yarn?

Use this table to decode labels on the spectrum of organic fibers available.

"MADE WITH"	"FULLY ORGANIC"	"RAISED ORGANIC"	"ORGANIC FIBERS"	"100% ORGANIC"
✓ Organically farmed	✓ Organically farmed	✓ Organically farmed	✓ Organically farmed	✓ Organically farmed
	✓ Pesticide-free grazing	✓ Pesticide-free grazing	✓ Pesticide-free grazing	✓ Pesticide-free grazing
		✓ Hand-spun	✓ Hand-spun	✓ Hand-spun
			✓ Naturally processed	✓ Naturally processed
				✓ Fully washed

Some Fiber Basics

All natural yarns are made from either plant or animal fibers. Fibers that come from animals are protein fibers. Fibers from plants are vegetable fibers, also known as cellulose. (Non-natural fibers are usually petroleum-based.)

To help you understand the difference among these fibers, think about the hundreds of types of fiber there are—ranging from very fine to coarse and kinky—and the wide range of colors in which they come. With the many species of animals and plants that exist, there are even more possibilities for variation.

The raw materials, the fibers, used in yarns have a very small diameter; this diameter is measured in "microns." When the fibers are smaller in diameter, they tend to feel softer against your skin and the "itch" or "prickle" factor is reduced. In general, the finer the fiber (thus lower micron measurement), the softer and less itchy the yarn. When a very soft fiber is spun and used to knit a garment, the garment will be light in weight. For instance, the fiber from cashmere measures about 15 microns. When it is spun, the resulting garment (and the yarn from which it is knit) is sinfully soft and light as a feather. At 11 microns, vicuna (see page 78) is the finest fiber, even finer than a single strand of a spider's web and virtually impossible to see with the naked eye. Fiber from the average baby alpaca is 22 microns, while superfine alpaca is about 26 microns.

Wool ranges from about 15 to 70 microns. However, New Zealander shepherds Kay and Garry Wilson recently raised an extraordinary sheep whose fiber measured 11.8 microns. This sheep was the culmination of the Wilsons' program of breeding for fine fiber. They cover their sheep with coats to protect the valuable fleece, feed them a diet of natural grains and hay, and even play music for the animals to keep them calm and peaceful.

The Patterns in *The Natural Knitter*

The focus of this book is knitting with natural fibers. While we have tried to make the directions for the patterns in this book as explicit as possible, we assume that you have a basic understanding of knitting and finishing techniques. There are many good basic books you can turn to for information on specific techniques. For additional help, see Knitting & Yarn Resources.

Little Sit-sters

DESIGNED BY JANET SCANLON

Janet says most knitters like to "sit and share a good yarn." In honor of some fabulous natural fibers, Janet made this village of charming and personable dolls. Frequently, she gives one of her creations to someone who might need a little friend.

You can knit a hidden pocket in a child's sweater and include one of these dolls as a special treat. Here, Janet provides a wide assortment of personalities to choose from so you can select the design that best fits your recipient.

Skill Level	Yarn	Needles & Notions		Gauge
Easy	• 20 to 30yd/18 to 28m of worsted weight or a medium weight yarn for each doll	• One set (3) each sizes 2 and 3 (2.75 and 3.25mm) double-pointed needles (dpns) *or size needed to obtain gauge.* (note: 4"/10 cm flexible sock needles are ideal for this project.)	• 18"/45cm length of pipe cleaner or flexible coated wire for each doll • Tapestry needle • Stiff cardboard for winding tassels • Beads and bells as specified	6 to 7 sts = 1"/2.5cm over St st (i.e., separated double knit sts—see below) using larger body needle. *Adjust needle sizes as necessary to obtain gauge.*

Note: Each "sit-ster" gives name and color of yarn(s) used for the project. Any medium-weight yarn of similar fiber content and color can be substituted.

• Scraps of novelty yarn for hair tassels

Silk Alpaca

Angora

Spindled

Qiviut

Alpaca

Tzarina

Construction Note

All pieces are worked in double knit, which is a method of creating a seamless St st tube with only 2 needles.

GLOSSARY

⊠ Separating stitches from 1 to 2 needles

Alternately, one at a time, slip all front (knit) stitches to one needle and all back (slipped) sts to a 2nd needle.

⊠ Putting stitches back on 1 needle

Slip one st from 1st needle to 3rd needle (front st), then slip one st from 2nd needle to 3rd needle (back st). Continue to alternate slipping sts from 1st and 2nd needles to 3rd needle in this manner.

DOUBLE KNIT

Pattern row On an even number of stitches work, *k1, sl 1 wyif; rep from * to end. Rep Pat Row for Double Knit.

Basic Sit-ster Instructions

Arms

Both arms are knit as one piece. Cut a 6"/15.5cm length of pipe cleaner. Make a ½"/1.5cm bend in each end and fold it back on itself. Wrap both ends with yarn so no sharp wire is exposed; set aside. Using smaller needles and yarn indicated, CO 6 sts. Work 5"/12.5cm of Double Knit. Separate sts onto 2 needles. Insert pipe cleaner into the arms. Return the stitches to a single needle (beginning with a front stitch, then alternating front and back). BO.

Legs

Fold a 12"/30cm length of pipe cleaner in half. Make a bend in each end as for the arms; set aside. Using larger needles, CO 6 sts for the first leg. Double knit for 3"/7.5cm. Cut yarn, leaving a 4"/10cm tail and set aside. Make a second leg, but do not cut the yarn. Slip both legs onto the same needle with working yarn to the right and the yarn tail of the first leg in the middle.

Body

Double knit the body for 1½"/4cm. Separate sts onto 2 needles. Insert one half of the pipe cleaner into each leg through the "neck" opening. (The fold in the pipe cleaner should be just below

the needles.) Lightly stuff the body with matching colored yarn.

Head

With sts still on separate needles, dec front sts for head as folls: ssk, k2, k2tog—4 sts. Rep for back sts. Put sts back on 1 needle—8 sts. Double knit the head for 1½"/4cm. Separate head sts onto 2 needles and lightly stuff with a small yarn ball of a matching color. Cut yarn, leaving a 6"/15cm tail. Using a tapestry needle, thread the tail through all the stitches twice to close the top of the head.

Finishing

Insert the arms through the body directly above the decrease round (enlarging the opening, if necessary) and tack into place. Weave in all ends. Embellish the head with a hair tassel, as directed.

Meet the Sit-sters...

Note: Follow Basic Sit-ster instructions unless directed otherwise.

PINK RIBBON SIT-STER

Yarn

SILK GARDEN by Noro (45% silk/45% kid mohair/10% wool)
• #43 Pink/Turquoise or any colorway with pink as dominant color

Notion

• One 6mm pink pearl

Follow basic Sit-ster instructions using Silk Garden yarn.

Arms

Using a pink section of the yarn, double knit st for 6½"/16.5cm. Do not add pipe cleaner.

Legs, body, and head

Follow Basic Sit-ster instructions. When the doll is finished, tack the arms together at the hands in the form of a Breast Cancer Awareness ribbon. Tuck the "knees" up into the arms.

Hair tassel

Overtwist the tail used to close the head. Thread pink pearl onto it and let it twist back on itself. Secure the end.

Left to right
Phat Sit-ster, Pink
Ribbon Sit-ster,
Mohair Sit-ster,
Tweedy Sit-ster.

SPINDLED SIT-STER

Yarn

FOXFIBRE by Vreseis Ltd. (100% organic cotton)
• ½oz/14g in Brown
SILK BOUCLÉ by Habu Textiles (100% silk boucle yarn)
• 30"/76cm in #31 for hair tassel

Notions

• Two small copper dancing bells

Follow basic Sit-ster instructions using cotton yarn.

Hair tassel

Thread 2 copper dancing bells onto a 24"/60cm length of silk boucle yarn. Wrap yarn around a 1½"/4cm square of cardboard 6 times. Place the bells where you want them and tie the yarn at one edge of the cardboard. Removing one loop at a time, overtwist it with your fingers and thumb until it curls around itself. Do this with each loop (2 loops will have bells on the ends). Sew tassel to top of head.

SIT-STER TZARINA

Yarn

FOREVER RANDOM FINE OBVERSE BLEND by La Lana Wools (60% Romney wool/40% yearling mohair)
• Tzarina

Notions

• Felted yarn scraps
• Two small copper dancing bells

Follow basic Sit-ster instructions using Forever Random Tzarina yarn.

Hair tassel

Twist together a few lengths of feltable yarn 18"/45cm long as folls: Wet your hands with warm water, apply a drop of dish detergent to your palms, and vigorously rub the wet fibers between your hands, re-wetting as needed to form a felted tangle of yarn. Rinse the yarn thoroughly. Cut into eight 1½–2"/4–5cm lengths. Let dry. Prepare a 4"/10cm length of yarn with a bell tied to each end. Fold this in half and sew it together with the felted pieces to form a tassel. Sew tassel to top of head.

QIVIUT SIT-STER

Note Qiviut yarns are available commercially (see Knitting & Yarn Resources).

Yarn

QIVIUT FOR 3-PLY HANDSPUN YARN (100% qiviut muskox)

• .3oz/9g in Natural
• Mixture of textured yarns for hair tassel

Follow basic Sit-ster instructions using qiviut yarn.

Hair tassel

Cut 12"/30cm lengths of each textured yarn. Make loops by wrapping them around a 1½"/4cm piece of cardboard. Tie them together at one edge. Remove the loops from the cardboard and cut the loops open. Trim and fluff the tassel and sew it to top of head.

SILK/ALPACA SIT-STER

Yarn

SILK/ALPACA BLEND FIBER FOR 2-PLY
HANDSPUN YARN
• ½oz/14g in Natural Brown
BOMBYX SILK FOR HANDSPUN YARN
• ¼oz/7g in Natural

Follow basic Sit-ster instructions using Silk Alpaca and silk yarns.

Arms

Using silk yarn, follow basic sit-ster instructions.

Legs, body, and head

Using silk/alpaca yarn, follow basic sit-ster instructions.

Tweedy Silk Sit-ster

Hair tassel

Cut a 24"/60cm length of silk yarn. Overtwist it. Make loops by holding the yarn under tension and wrapping it around a 1½"/4cm piece of cardboard. Tie them together at one edge. Remove the loops from the cardboard one at a time, letting them twist back on themselves to form plied braids. Sew tassel to top of head.

PHAT SILK SIT-STER

Yarn

PHAT SILK FINE by La Lana Wools (50% Bombyx silk/50% fine wool)
• Yellow

Notions

• Multicolored metallic embroidery thread
• Three small gold dancing bells
• Two ½"/13mm glass leaf beads

Follow basic Sit-ster instructions using Phat Silk yarn.

Arms and Body

Holding 1 strand of Phat Silk and 1 strand of embroidery thread together, follow basic sit-ster instructions.

Hair tassel

String 2 glass leaves and 3 gold bells onto a 24"/60cm length of embroidery thread. Overtwist the thread and ply it back on itself, placing the bells and beads along the twist. Pull on each bell and bead lightly to form individual twisted loops along the length of the thread. Gather loops together, forming a tassel. Sew tassel to top of head.

ALPACA SIT-STER

Yarn

INCA ALPACA by Classic Elite (100% alpaca)
• #1131 Blue Danube (A) and #1135
Cala Cala Moss (B)
CHARM by Trendsetter Yarns (77% polyester/23% polyamide Tactel)
• 2yds/2m in #1480 Jungle River (C)

Arms

Work 2½"/6.5cm in A, then [2 rows B, 2 rows A] 8 times. Follow basic sit-ster instructions to end.

Body

Work 1 st leg with B and set aside. Work 2nd leg as folls: [4 rows B, 4 rows A] 4 times, ending with 4 rows B. Cut B. Knit across both legs using A. Follow basic sit-ster body instructions.

Hair tassel

Wrap C around your fingers making 12 loops, each 2"/5cm long. Tie the bundle at the center and slip the loops off your fingers. Separate to form a loopy halo (makes 24 loops). Sew tassel to top of head.

MOHAIR SIT-STER

Yarn

MOUNTAIN GOAT by Mountain Colors (55% mohair/45% wool)
• Golden Willow
TURINO SILK by Plymouth Yarns (100% raw silk)
• 1yd/1m each in #01 and #02

Follow basic Sit-ster instructions using mohair yarn.

Hair tassel

Cut 4 strands of silk, each 8"/20cm long. Tie 4 small overhand knots close together then tie another knot over the top of these, making a larger knot. Rep this 2 or 3 times for each strand. Overtwist each strand and let it twist back on itself, forming a plied braid. Tie the ends of the braids together to make a tassel. Sew tassel to top of head.

ANGORA SIT-STER

Yarn

ANGEL by Lorna's Laces (70% angora/30% lambswool)
• #204 Daffodil

Follow basic Sit-ster instructions using Angel yarn.

Hair tassel

Cut a 36"/90cm length of yarn. Overtwist it. Make loops by holding the yarn under tension and wrapping it around a 2"/5cm form. Tie them together at one edge. Remove the loops from the form one at a time, letting them twist back on themselves to form plied braids. Sew tassel to top of head.

TWEEDY SILK SIT-STER

Yarn

SHINANO by Noro (65% wool/35% silk)
• #10 Red/Turquoise

Follow basic Sit-ster instructions using Shinano yarn.

Arms and body

Follow basic sit-ster instructions, leaving a 12"/30cm long tail after gathering the head stitches.

Hair tassel

Overtwist the 12"/30cm tail. Let it twist back on itself to form a plied braid. Fold into three strands and secure.

Chapter 1
FROM SHEEP TO WOOL

When it comes to knitting, sheep are knitters' best friends. Their covering of thick hair, called fleece, is cleaned and processed into wool. Wool is warm, elastic, durable, flame retardant (according to *The Principles of Knitting*, it is used for clothing worn by firefighters and for the blankets they use to smother flames), and takes dyes easily. You can bend wool and it will spring back to its original shape. Wool will resist wrinkles. When spun with other nonelastic fibers, wool will lend these great properties to the yarn, which results in a more structured garment. It is perfect partnered with some specialty fibers (such as llama, alpaca, and cashmere) that tend to droop a bit when used alone.

Opposite
Depending on how the fleece of the speckled Jacobs Sheep is spun, you can get many varieties of yarn. It can be separated into all white or all dark, or corded together.

For insulating, wool is excellent. It is warm when the temperature is cold and stays fairly cool when it is hot out. This marvelous feature is attributed to its crimp. Crimp is the reoccurrence of corrugation in a fiber. Crimp creates little air pockets between the fibers, and this prevents the fibers from packing together.

Wool is also slightly water repellent. It can absorb up to one-third its weight in water before it starts to feel wet. In fact, a wool garment will float for a while. Wool is a protein fiber and composed of keratin. Each fiber is made up of an outer membrane, the cuticle, and an inner portion, the cortex. The cortex determines the shape of the fiber. Overlapping scales cover the cuticle (sort of like shingles) and hold the fiber together. Because of these overlapping scales, wool will felt if it is subjected to moisture, heat, and friction. Sometimes you may want felting to occur, and other times, this is the ruination of a favorite sweater.

Allergies to Wool

Many people believe they are allergic to wool. However, a true allergy to wool is extremely rare. A coarse wool, typically used to weave a carpet, would indeed feel scratchy if it were worn against the skin. But if someone finds wool irritating, this could be because miniscule bits of grass were left in the fleece before it was spun, or because of the type of soap or spinning oils that were used during processing. Naturally produced wool helps keep the skin dry and warm, unlike some synthetic fibers that can hold in moisture and irritate skin.

There are hundreds of sheep breeds and they all produce wool with their own distinct traits and characteristics. The fleece colors can range from white through all the shades of gray and brown to black. In some cases, all these shades exist on the same animal! The length of the fleece can range from one inch to eighteen inches. The wool produced can vary from being very fine, and great for making knitting yarns for soft garments, to coarser, and used to make items such as wool rugs. In general, the fleeces from lambs tends to be finer.

To obtain the fleece from the sheep, several methods have been used. The oldest method is "rooing," which is running your hands through the fleece on the sheep and gathering the loose strands. Older breeds of sheep used to shed and there would be "wool gathering" in which the "harvesters" would gather the bits and pieces of wool that got entangled in fences and bushes. Of course, the most common and efficient method is shearing. Most sheep are sheared in the springtime. The shorn fiber is cleaned by scouring it in a detergent bath that removes vegetable matter and lanolin. The scoured fleece is then spun into fibers.

Right
Overflowing from its container, wool fleece for spinning your own yarn is shown for sale.

Opposite
These recently shorn sheep—without their customary wool "coats"—warm themselves in the sun at the Maryland Sheep and Wool Festival, which takes place every year in the spring.

Have you ever wondered what virgin wool is? It is wool that has never been processed, woven, or knitted, as opposed to wool that has been previously processed, taken apart, and respun into a new fiber.

Shrek the Sheep

In April 2004, a nine-year-old merino sheep was finally captured after spending six years roaming the hills of Central Otago, New Zealand. Once a member of a herd, this very fluffy fellow decided to take a walk on the wild side. He had a fifty-nine-pound fleece (the average sheep fleece weighs two to four pounds). His capture made international news and he was named Shrek after the ogre in the Dreamworks movie of the same name. Personal appearances and the sales of his fleece raised money for a charitable New Zealand foundation, Cure Kids (www.curekids.org.nz).

Shrek is now shorn regularly, but dons a special merino jacket made by a New Zealand–based merino apparel company, to ensure that he is insulated from extreme weather conditions.

Daydream: Knitter's Meditation Mat & Bag

DESIGNED BY JANET SCANLON

The stripes in Daydream flow with an easy rhythm. Raised spirals wind around the knitted tube, creating a subtle texture. Each end of the mat reflects the other, meeting in the center.

The double-thick mat is comfortable to lie on and becomes a sitting cushion when folded in thirds and tucked into itself. Carry or store the rolled mat in its net bag. Knitted with soft woolen-spun yarn, the tube will felt 20–25 percent into a lofty fabric.

Caution: This is not an exercise mat.

Skill Levels
Meditation Mat Intermediate; *Carrying Bag* Intermediate

Finished Measurements
Meditation Mat
Circumference 56"/142cm
Length 72"/183cm

Carrying Bag
Circumference 16"/40.5cm
Length 32"/81.25cm

Yarn
PHILOSOPHER'S WOOL 3-PLY, 4oz/114g skeins, each approx 150yd/135m (100% wool) or a bulky weight yarn

Note: The following amounts include enough yarn to make the meditation mat and the carrying bag. If you substitute yarns, swatch and full before beginning the project to test fullability of your yarn.

• 4 skeins each in Dark Green Heather (A), Jade (B), Brown Heather (D), and Dark Blue Heather (H)

• 3 skeins in Peat (C)

• 2 skeins each in Forest (E), Navy (F), Grape (G), and Dark Purple Heather (I)

• 1 skein in Light Purple Heather (J)

Needles & Notions
• Size 10½ (6.5mm) circular needles, 24"/60cm and 29"/73.5 cm long *or size needed to obtain gauge*

• One set (4) each sizes 8, 10, and 10½ (5, 6, and 6.5mm) double-pointed needles (dpns) *or size needed to obtain gauge*

• Size H/8 (5mm) crochet hook

• Stitch marker

• Safety pin marker

• Tapestry needle

• 5" x 3"/12.5 x 7.5cm piece of stiff cardboard for winding tassels

Gauges
Meditation Mat
12 sts and 16 rnds = 4"/10cm over St st using size 10½ (6.5mm) dpns (before fulling). *Adjust needle size as necessary to obtain correct gauge.*

Carrying Bag
5.5 sts and 8 rows = 4"/10cm in double knit stitch using size 10½ (6.5mm) dpns (measuring one side of fabric when taken off the needle). Exact gauge is not critical for this project.

Construction Notes:

MEDITATION MAT

1) This mat is knit as a huge horizontal-striped tube with twisted-stitch stripes spiraling at an angle down the length of the tube. These stripes and spirals mirror each other at the center.

2) The horizontal stripes are worked with the yarn attached to the ball; the twisted-stitch spirals are worked with separate lengths of yarn.

3) Be careful when knitting a horizontal stripe and spiral of the same color to make sure that the stripe is knit from the ball and the spiral is knit from the separate length.

4) The six spirals are set up in the first 9"/22.5cm of the tube. Note that the spirals are begun out of sequence as folls: Spirals 1 and 4 are worked in A, Spiral 2 is worked in B, Spirals 3 and 6 are worked in A, and Spiral 5 is worked in B. Work Spirals as you come to them on all rounds, weaving in yarn tails as you go.

CARRYING BAG

1) This bag is worked in a method of double knitting that gives a net-like twisted stitch.

2) When the bag is the desired length, the stitches are separated onto 2 needles (front and back), then put onto a circular needle to bind off for an open top.

GLOSSARY

※ **Left Twist (LT)** Knit into the back loop of the 2nd st on left needle and leave on needle; then knit into the back loops of both the 1st and 2nd sts and slip both sts tog to right-hand needle.

※ **Spiral st** Work to Spiral st from previous rnd; with main color, k1tbl; then with Spiral yarn, work LT. Drop Spiral st color and cont with stripe color.

※ **Color Change rnd** Work Spiral 1, then with new color, [k1, sl 1] around, working Spiral sts as you come to them.

INSTRUCTIONS FOR THE MEDITATION MAT

With longer circular needle and C, CO on 200 sts. Join, taking care not to twist sts on needle. Pm to indicate beg of rnd and sl marker every rnd.

Rnds 1–7 With C, knit. Cut yarn.

Rnd 8 (Color Change) Join A, *K1, sl 1; rep from * around.

Rnds 9–10 With A, knit. Cut yarn.

Set up spirals

(beg Spirals 1 and 4)

Color Change rnd Join D, k1. Beg Spiral 1 as folls: join a length of A, work LT, then drop A; cont with D, k1, *sl 1, k1; rep from * for a total of 66 sts. Beg Spiral 4 as folls: join another length of A, work LT, then drop A; cont with D, *k1, sl 1; rep from * to Spiral 1. Remove beg of rnd marker. Spiral 1 is the new beg of rnd. Mark with a safety pin, moving it up as needed.

Next rnd *With D, k1 into back of first st of Spiral 1, drop D, with A, work LT, drop A (Spiral st made)*. With D, knit to Spiral 4; rep Spiral st instructions from * to *; with D, knit to Spiral 1.

Next 4 rnds With D, knit, working Spiral sts as you come to them (the spirals will shift one st to the left on each rnd).

Color Change rnd Work Spiral 1; cut D and join B; *k1, sl 1; rep from * around, working Spiral 4 as you come to it. With B, knit next rnd.

Next rnd (beg Spiral 2) Work Spiral 1; with B, k5 sts; attach separate length of B, work LT (Spiral 2), drop length of B; cont with main yarn B and knit, working Spiral 4 as you come to it.

Next 5 rnds With D, work Color Change rnd, then knit 4 rnds, working Spirals as you come to them.

Next 2 rnds With A, work Color Change rnd, then knit 1 rnd, working Spirals as you come to them.

Next rnd (beg Spirals 3 and 6) With D, work Color Change rnd, AT THE SAME TIME, with lengths of A, begin Spiral 3 eight sts past Spiral 2, and Spiral 6 sixteen sts past Spiral 4.

Next 4 rnds With D, knit, working Spirals as you come to them.

Next 2 rnds With B, work Color Change rnd, then knit one rnd, working spirals as you come to them.

Next 5 rnds (beg Spiral 5) With D, work Color Change rnd, AT THE SAME TIME, with length of B, begin Spiral 5 ten sts past Spiral 4, then knit 4 rnds, working Spirals as you come to them. The 6 spirals are set up. Work Spirals as you come to them on each round, adding extra lengths of yarn as needed.

Horizontal stripes

Working Rnd 1 of each stripe as a Color Change rnd and cont to work spirals as they present themselves, work horizontal stripes as folls (the number indicates *total* number of rounds per color): 8 rnds E, 3 rnds C, 6 rnds E, 8 rnds C, 4 rnds A, 9 rnds D, 8 rnds A, 3 rnds F, 11 rnds A, 8 rnds F, 4 rnds G, 5 rnds F, 7 rnds G, 2 rnds H, 5 rnds G, 7 rnds H, 3 rnds I, 8 rnds H, 7 rnds I, 2 rnds B, 10 rnds I, 7 rnds H, 3 rnds J, 4 rnds H, and 7 rnds J. This is the center of the mat.

Second half of mat

The second half of the mat is a mirror image. The stripe sequence is worked in reverse from the center to the first stripe. To mirror the end of Spirals with the beg, end the appropriate Spirals on the starred stripes as folls: 4 rnds H, 3 rnds J, 7 rnds H, 10 rnds I, 2 rnds B, 7 rnds I, 8 rnds H, 3 rnds I, 7 rnds H, 5 rnds G, 2 rnds H, 7 rnds G; 5 rnds F, 4 rnds G, 8 rnds F, 11 rnds A, 3 rnds F, 8 rnds A, 9 rnds D, 4 rnds A, 8 rnds C, 6 rnds E, 3 rnds C, 8 rnds E, 5 rnds D, 2 rnds B, 5 rnds D, 2 rnds A, 5 rnds D, 3 rnds B, 5 rnds D, 3 rnds A, and 7 rnds C.

FINISHING

With a tapestry needle, weave in loose yarn tails to the WS of work and secure.

Fulling the mat

Fulling is when a knitted item is washed in hot water, whereas felting is when the unspun fiber is worked together by hand to form a thick fabric. Fill the washing machine with hot water; add a small amount of dishwashing detergent. Insert the mat. Set machine to low speed, resetting the timer for several cycles, as necessary. If the water becomes cool, remove the mat and refill the machine. Return the mat to the washer and continue to agitate on low speed until the fabric is fulled (i.e., until the stitches are obscured). The slow agitation promotes uniform fulling while preventing twisting and creasing. Thoroughly rinse the mat in warm water; DO NOT SPIN! Remove the mat from the washer and lay flat, smoothing the mat into shape. Allow the mat to dry thoroughly, rotating it several times to prevent side creases from forming.

INSTRUCTIONS FOR THE CARRYING BAG

With longer circular needle and B, CO 32 sts. Do not join. Work back and forth in double-knitting stitch as folls:

PHILOSOPHER'S WOOL

IN 1986, EUGENE AND ANN BOURGEOIS STARTED PHILOSOPHER'S WOOL WITH THE MISSION OF improving the price farmers received for their fleeces. The Bourgeoises were convinced that they would receive high-quality fleeces if they paid the farmers decently for the wool. As a farmer, Eugene said, "I was often bemused at how soft the fleece was on the sheep, but how harsh it became when it was made into a sweater." The washing mill thoroughly scoured the wool to remove vegetable matter in the fleece and, ironically, then added moisturizers to soften the wool. The Bourgeoises wanted to retain the natural oils of the wool and avoid the chemicals, acids, and bleaches that were routinely used when wool was washed. They believed that these processes dehydrated the wool and made it scratchy and itchy.

Philosopher's Wool rewards farmers who produce clean fleeces. While it is time-consuming, most farmers realize that it is worth the effort to keep the sheep clean and produce strong, high-quality wool.

In addition to doing "the right thing" by the farmer, Philosopher's Wool has also come up with wonderful palettes of yarn. These categories are based on their imagined view of the world. For The Knitter's Meditation Mat, designer Janet Scanlon selected colors from the Woodland and Peacock categories.

Row 1 *Yo, k1, pass the yo over the k1, sl 1 wyib; rep from * to end. Rep Row 1 until bag measures 32"/81.5cm from beg. Separate the stitches onto 2 10½" (6.5mm) dpns, slipping the odd-numbered sts (front sts) to one needle and the even-numbered sts (back sts) to the other. This separates the two halves of the bag, creating the top opening. Now, slip them back onto the 24"/60cm long circular needle, taking care to align them correctly.

Eyelet rnd With crochet hook and yarn still attached to knitting, * work sl st in first st on needle, drop st from needle, ch 5; rep from * until all stitches are bound off. To join rnd, ch 5, sc in first sl st. Fasten off.

Twisted draw cord

Cut six 7yd/6.5m lengths of B. Knot them together at each end. Secure one end to a doorknob and insert a knitting needle into the other end. Keeping the strands taut, twist the cord counterclockwise until it begins twisting back on itself. Remove the needle and fold the cord in half, bringing the knotted ends together. (**Hint:** Position a chair about halfway to the doorknob and use it as the "folding point." This will help you maintain tension on the cord and will keep the two halves from twisting together before you are ready.) Reinsert the knitting needle at the fold and twist clockwise, plying the 2 strands back on themselves. Slowly release the tension and the cord will continue to twist. Smooth out any kinks with your hands. Beg at one side of the bag, thread the cord in and out through alternating eyelets.

Splice the cord ends

Cut the knot off the one end, then pass this end through the loop at the other end of the cord, abutting the two pieces for about 3"/7.5cm. Separate strands of the cut end and weave them, one at a time, into the cord for about 1½"/4cm. Trim excess.

Wrap the splice

Cut a 30"/76cm length of yarn to make the cord. Fold one end into a 2½"/6.5cm loop and lay this loop along the cord covering the splice, with about ½"/1.5cm extending beyond the splice. Wrap the other end of the piece of yarn around the loop evenly for 2"/5cm, moving toward the fold. Insert the wrapping end of the yarn through the loop end. Gently pull on the opposite end of the loop to draw it into the wrap. To prevent any wraps from slipping off the end of the cord, pass the remaining yarn tail around the wrap (vertically binding it). Thread the tail into a darning needle and tack it to the center of the wrap with a couple of small sts. Weave in loose ends. Trim to neaten. Make an overhand knot 18"/45.5cm from the spliced end of the draw cord. This forms a 32"/81cm loop that slips over the bottom of the bag (and mat), thus creating a shoulder strap for carrying.

INSTRUCTIONS FOR THE FELTED BEAD TASSELS (3 long and 2 short tassels)

Beads

With smallest dpns and colors of your choice, work three 2-st I-cords, each 9"/23cm long. With middle-sized dpns and colors of your choice, work three 3-st I-cords, each 12"/30.5 cm long. With largest dpns and colors of your choice, work three 5-st I-cords, each 15"/38cm long. Create 3 tubes, each with 3 layers of color, by inserting the smallest I-cords into the medium I-cords, then the medium I-cords into the largest ones, layering the colors as you choose.

Felt the beads

Roll each tube vigorously between your palms in warm, soapy water until the tubes feel solid. Cut the felted tubes into ¾"/2cm segments; let these pieces float in warm water until needed. Roll two or three segments at a time between wet soapy hands until they become firm round beads. Rinse repeatedly and squeeze out excess water. Roll the beads on a towel to remove more moisture and smooth the bead surface. Set the beads aside to dry thoroughly.

Long tassel fringes (make 3)

Cut a 10'/3m length of B and twist it tightly until it kinks, then fold it in half making a 2-plied twisted cord. Using a large-eyed sharp needle, pierce the centers of 7 beads and thread onto the cord. Slide the beads randomly spaced along the cord and wrap the cord 4 times around a 5"/12.5cm piece of cardboard to make tassel fringes. Tie the tassel fringes together as folls: make a 15"/38cm 2-plied twisted cord with B. Fold this cord in half and tie an overhand knot 1½"/4cm from the fold, forming a loop and leaving 2 tails 5–6"/12.5–15cm long. Place the knot against the wraps at one edge of the cardboard.

Use the tails to tie a square knot around the 4 strands of tassel fringe. Remove the tassel from the cardboard. Wrap the neck of the tassel for 1½"/4cm.

Short tassels (make 2)

Make an 18"/45cm 2-ply twisted cord with B. Follow the instructions above, stringing it with 3 beads and wrapping it around a 3"/7.5cm cardboard 2 times for tassels. Tie and wrap them as for the long tassels.

Attach the tassels

Pull the top loop through the fabric with a crochet hook and pass the beaded fringe through this loop. Attach the short tassels to the bottom corners of the net bag, two of the long tassels at the bottom corners of the mat and one at the spliced end of the twisted draw cord. The tassels can be removed or repositioned.

Shetland Fern

DESIGNED BY JENNIFER LINDSAY

This design is based on ferns Jennifer observed growing in a meadow on St. Ninian's, a tiny island just off Shetland's Mainland island in Scotland. She "was charmed by their finely cut leaves, and luxuriant, swirling growth habit which belies the harshness of their North Sea habitat. Each square of leaves echoes the Norwegian star patterns."

When viewed from a distance, the design explodes into a large and dramatic OXO pattern, a traditional Shetland motif whose origins and significance are still under debate.

"Shetland Fern" is created using Shetland 2000 Yarn—an all-natural, undyed Shetland wool available in nine shades and perfect for replicating the natural fern motif.

Skill Level

Experienced

Sizes

Instructions are for Size 1 (X-Small/Small). Changes for Size 2 (Medium/Large) are in parentheses. Shown in Size 1.

Finished Measurements

Bust 40½ (48)"/103 (122)cm
Length 24¼"/61.5cm
Sleeve length 19 (19½)"/48 (49.5)cm

Yarn

SHETLAND 2000 by Yarns International, 1¾oz/50g skeins, each approx 190yd/174m (100% Shetland wool) or a fine weight yarn
• 6 (8) skeins in #2001 Shetland White (A)
• 3 skeins in #2002 Mooskit (B)
• 3 (4) skeins in #2003 Shaela (C)
• 2 (3) skeins in #2004 Moorit (D)
• 2 skeins in #2005 Shetland Black (E)

Needles & Notions

• Sizes 1 and 2 (2.25 and 3mm) circular needles, 32"/80cm long *or size needed to obtain gauge*
• Size 1 (2.25mm) circular needle, 24"/60cm long
• Size 2 (3mm) circular needle, 16"/40cm long
• One set (4) each sizes 1 and 2 (2 and 2.25mm) double-pointed needles (dpns)
• Stitch markers
• Safety pins
• Sharp scissors
• Tapestry needle

Gauge

34 sts and 34 rows = 4"/10cm over Shetland Fern patt using larger needle. *Adjust the needle size as necessary to obtain correct gauge.*

Note: This sweater is knitted very densely. If you want more of a range of sizes than those offered here, adjust your gauge to 33 sts and 33 rows = 4"/10cm to obtain a bust that measures 41 (49½)"/104 (125.5)cm. Or, 32 sts and 32 rows = 4"/10cm to obtain a bust that measures 42½ (51)"/108 (129.5)cm. Finished lengths will also increase approx 1"/2.5cm for each change in gauge. The yarn knits nicely at looser gauges, but some of the crisp detail of the pattern may be lost, and yarn requirements will differ somewhat from those listed.

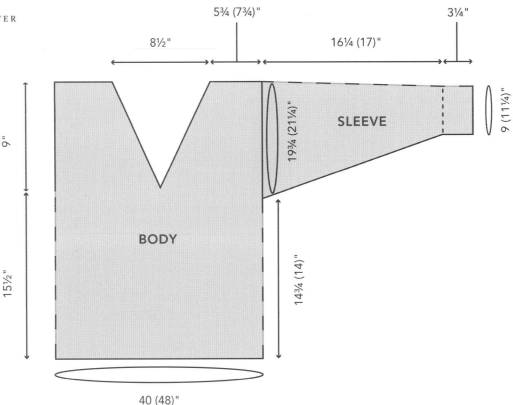

8½"

5¾ (7¾)"

16¼ (17)"

3¼"

9"

19¾ (21¼)"

SLEEVE

15½"

14¾ (14)"

BODY

9 (11¼)"

40 (48)"

Construction Notes

1) This sweater is worked in the round from the bottom up using Fair Isle techniques; steeks (extra stitches) are added at the armholes and V-neck and are cut when the body is finished.

2) The shoulders are joined using 3-needle bind-off.

3) The sleeves are picked up from the armholes and worked from the top down in the round, working the color stitch pattern chart upside down.

4) The collar is worked last, with stitches picked up around the V-neck, from which a ribbed collar stand is worked back and forth using short-row shaping.

5) The foldover collar is worked in a Fair Isle stitch pattern and finished with a 2-color edging.

GLOSSARY

▓ **steek** Stitches that are cast on, then later cut to create armholes or V-neck. These sts are worked in a checkerboard fashion.

▓ **edge sts** One st on each side of steek. Always worked with A.

▓ **edge st and steek cast on** Backwards loop (e-wrap) cast-on.

▓ **sm** Slip marker.

▓ **3-needle bind-off** Holding needles parallel with RS together and WS facing, k2tog from front and back needles, *k2tog from front and back needles and pass the first st over the second to bind off; rep from * to end.

INSTRUCTIONS FOR THE BODY

With smaller, 32" circular needle and E, CO 340 (400) sts. Join, taking care not to twist sts on needle. Pm to indicate beg of rnd and sl marker every rnd. Work around in k2, p2 rib for 4 rnds, inc 2 (dec 1) st on last rnd—342 (399) sts. With D, knit 1 rnd, then purl 2 rnds. Change to larger, 32" circular needle and St st.

Beg Chart A

Rnd 1 Work 19-st rep 18 (21) times. Cont work to Rnd 18. With D, knit 1 rnd, purl 1 rnd.

Mark side seams

For Size 1 only

Slip beg of rnd marker, p169, p2tog, pm, p169, p2tog—340 sts.

For Size 2 only

Slip beg of rnd marker, [M1, p45, M1, p44] twice, [M1, p44] 4 times, M1, p45, placing marker after st 204—408 sts.

Beg Chart B

Rnd 1 Beg at st indicated on chart. Cont to work to Rnd 36, then rep Rnds 1–36 once more, then Rnds 1–24 (1–19) once.

Set up armhole steeks

Rnd 25 (20) Before slipping beg of rnd marker, CO 1 edge st with A, then CO 4 steek sts alternating colors, sm, work in pat to 1 st before next marker, and place that st on a safety pin, sm, CO 1 edge st with A, then CO 8 steek sts alternating colors, CO 1 edge st with A, pm, work to last st before marker and place that st on a safety pin, sm, CO 1 edge st with A, CO 4 steek sts, alternating colors and working first steek st in A—358 (426) sts. You will have 169 (203) sts on the back and front of the body, separated by 2 edge and 8 steek sts at each armhole. Work even through Rnd 30, maintaining edge sts in A, and alternating colors for steek sts each rnd to create a checkerboard effect.

Set up V-neck steek

Rnd 31 Work to center front 3 sts (the 16th to-18th sts on chart) and place these sts on a safety pin, pm, CO 2 edge and 8 steek sts as for armholes, pm, work to end of rnd—365 (433) sts. You will have 83 (100) sts for right front, 10 V-neck steek and edge sts, 83 (100) sts for left front, 10 armhole steek and edge sts, 169 (203) sts for back, and 10 armhole steek and edge sts.

Neck shaping

Dec rnd Work to 2 sts before V-neck marker, ssk, sm, work edge and steek sts, sm, k2tog, work to end of rnd. Rep Dec rnd every other rnd 21 times more, then every 3rd rnd 11 times—50 (67) sts in each front section. Work even through Rnd 36.
Next rnd Work Rnd 1 of pat, binding off the steek sts at neck and armholes using alternating colors, but leaving all other sts, including the edge sts on the needles—50 (67) sts for right front, 2 V-neck edge sts, 50 (67) sts for left front, 2 armhole edge sts, 169 (203) sts, for back and 2 armhole edge sts.

CHART A

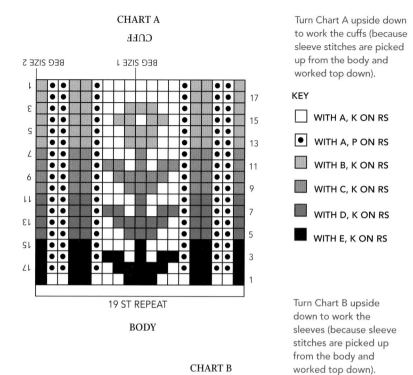

BODY

Turn Chart A upside down to work the cuffs (because sleeve stitches are picked up from the body and worked top down).

KEY

- ☐ WITH A, K ON RS
- ☐• WITH A, P ON RS
- ☐ WITH B, K ON RS
- ☐ WITH C, K ON RS
- ☐ WITH D, K ON RS
- ■ WITH E, K ON RS

Turn Chart B upside down to work the sleeves (because sleeve stitches are picked up from the body and worked top down).

CHART B

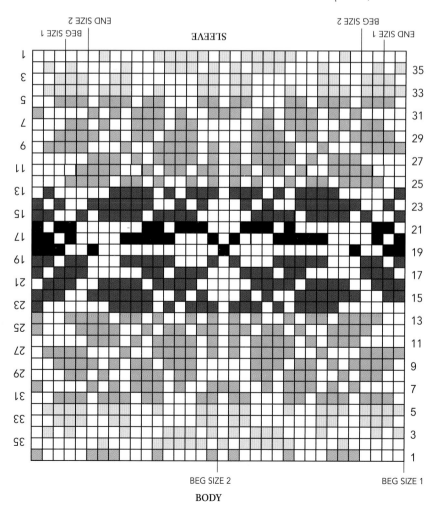

BODY

Join shoulder seams

Starting with the right front, slip 1 edge st from V-neck, 50 (67) sts from right front, and 1 edge st from armhole edge onto a spare needle. Slip 1 armhole edge st and 51 (68) sts from back onto another spare needle. Turn garment inside out and join back to front at shoulders using A, larger needle and 3-needle bindoff technique, removing any st markers that remain as you work across. Rep for left front. With A, BO rem 67 sts at back neck.

Cut open armhole steeks

Working one armhole at a time, mark a st close to the center of the steek to use as the cutting line. Using a sharp pair of scissors, carefully cut the steek in half following this line; the armhole of the sweater will open up, faced by raw edges of roughly equal width on either side.

INSTRUCTIONS FOR THE SLEEVES

With RS facing and using larger, 16" circular needle and A, slip underarm st from safety pin onto needle without working it; pick up and k 84 (89) sts between the edge sts and the main fabric up the front and then 84 (91) sts down the back, knitting the underarm st as the last of these 84 (91) sts—168 (180) sts. Pm to indicate beg of rnd. (**Note:** Always work the underarm st with A.) Purl 1 rnd with A. Cont in St st.
Beg Chart B
Turn chart upside-down.

Starting on Rnd 5 (1) of chart and beg at st indicated, work even for 2 rnds.
Dec rnd Ssk, work to last 3 sts, k2tog, k1A (underarm st). Rep Dec rnd every 4th rnd 0 (14) times more, then every 3rd rnd 45 (27) times more, changing to dpns when necessary—76 (96) sts.
For Size 2 only
Work even for 2 rnds, then dec one st at end of next rnd—95 sts.
For both sizes Work even until 4th rep of Rnd 36 is completed.

Cuff

Change to smaller dpns and D. Knit 1 rnd, then purl 2 rnds.
Beg Chart A
Turn chart upside-down.
Rnd 1 Knit, beg and end at sts indicated on chart. Cont in rib following chart Rnds 2–18. Change CC4 and knit 1 rnd, then purl 2 rnds.
Next (dec) rnd With E, knit around dec 8 (11) sts evenly spaced—68 (84) sts. Cont with E only and work in k2, p2 rib for 4 rnds. BO all sts loosely in rib.

INSTRUCTIONS FOR THE COLLAR

With RS facing, slip the 3 sts at the center front from the safety pin onto smaller, 24" circular needle. With D, knit these 3 sts, pm, pick up and k 79 sts to right shoulder, pm, pick up and k 67 sts along back neck, pm, pick up and k 78 sts from left shoulder to center front, pm—227 sts. Join and mark beg of rnd and sl marker every rnd or row. Purl next 2 rnds.

CHART C

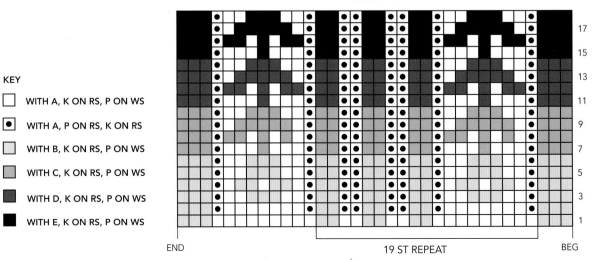

KEY

☐ WITH A, K ON RS, P ON WS

◉ WITH A, P ON RS, K ON RS

☐ WITH B, K ON RS, P ON WS

▨ WITH C, K ON RS, P ON WS

▨ WITH D, K ON RS, P ON WS

■ WITH E, K ON RS, P ON WS

END · · · 19 ST REPEAT · · · BEG

YARNS INTERNATIONAL

BONNIE HASSLER AND BETTY LINDSAY (DESIGNER JENNIFER'S MOTHER-IN-LAW) CO-OWN YARNS

International in Bethesda, Maryland. When Betty made her first trip to Shetland, she immersed herself in the culture of knitting—from the crofter farmers who raise the hardy native sheep to the knitters who use the wool to make their world famous Fair Isle garments and delicate Shetland lace shawls.

During Betty's visit to Jamieson and Smith (Shetland Wool Brokers) Limited of Lerwick, Oliver Henry, who oversees production there, mentioned with regret how the current demands for white yarn that could be easily dyed had adversely affected the population of naturally colored

Shetland sheep on the island. At that time, naturally colored Shetland yarns that were not overdyed were fast becoming a rarity and made only by handspinners who spun them for their own use. Yarns International joined forces with Jamieson and Smith to provide Shetland 2000™ in nine natural shades to a wider audience of knitters. Because of a minimum of processing it is very soft, and the natural saturation of the colors gives the knitted pieces a richness and depth unavailable from dyed yarns. As an added benefit, the crofters have an incentive to preserve the colored sheep because there is

now a market for their fleece and not just for their meat. Yarns International offers extensive pattern support for Shetland 2000™ yarn.

Next row (RS) With D, BO center 3 sts; on 4th st, change to E and knit to end of row—224 sts. Turn. Work in k1, p1 rib for 1 row.

Short rows

Working back and forth, shape collar stand as folls: *Work in k1, p1 rib as established to last 5 sts (or, on subsequent rows, to 5 sts before last wrapped st), wyif, slip the next st to RH needle, move yarn to back, wrapping the slipped st. Turn work and slip the wrapped st back to RH needle; rep from * (working 5 fewer sts each row) a total of 16 times—8 wrapped sts each side. (**Note:** It is helpful to mark each wrapped st with a safety pin so you can easily track how many short rows you have completed.)
Next row Work in rib all the way to the end, leaving wraps in position. Cont in rib across all sts for 3 rows—224 sts. With D, knit 2 rows, then purl 1 row.

Beg chart C

Next (collar turn) row (RS) Turn work, attach yarns and beg Chart C at opposite end of needle,

beg and end where indicated, working 12 reps of color st patt. Work even until Chart C is complete.

Edging

With RS of collar facing and D, beg at center front neck, pick up and k 23 sts along right front edge of collar, k224 collar sts, then pickup and k 23 sts along left front edge of collar—270 sts. With D, knit 1 row, then purl 1 row. With E, purl 1 row.
Next row (RS) K2, *p2, k2; rep from * to end. Cont in k2, p2 rib as established for 3 more rows. BO all sts loosely in rib.

FINISHING

Trim steek sts; tack down on the inside of the sweater using tapestry needle and single ply of yarn. Fold edges of collar closest to the V-neck opening to the inside of the sweater and tack them down so that D ridges meet neatly at the center of the V-neck. With tapestry needle, weave in loose yarn tails to the WS of work and secure. Steam or block garment into shape.

Ålvros Sweater

DESIGNED BY BETH BROWN-REINSEL

Beth's inspiration for this traditional sweater comes from Britt-Marie Christoffersson's book *Swedish Sweaters*. In this design, she uses motifs taken from a nineteenth-century garment from the town of Ålvros, Sweden, and punched it up with motifs of her own. The intarsia knit in the round keeps things interesting.

Unlike many ski sweaters, this one is very soft and snuggly and was designed and knit with the premium and very soft merino wool from Morehouse Farm.

Skill Level
Experienced

Sizes
Instructions are for Small. Changes for Medium and Large are in parentheses. Shown in size Medium.

Finished Measurements
Bust 39½ (44½, 49½)"/100.5 (113, 125.5)cm
Length 25¼"/64cm

Yarn
MOREHOUSE FARM MERINO 2-PLY, 2oz/56.75g skeins, each approx 220yd/201m (100% merino wool) or a light weight yarn

• 6 (8, 10) skeins in Black (A)

• 1 skein in Cranberry (B)

• 5 (7, 9) skeins in Soft White (C)

Needles & Notions
• Size 4 (3.5mm) circular needles, 16"/40cm and 32"/80cm long *or size needed to obtain gauge*

• One set (4) each sizes 2 and 4 (2.75 and 3.5mm) double-pointed needles (dpns)

• Stitch markers

• Stitch holders (or waste yarn)

• Tapestry needle

• Sewing machine

Gauge
28 sts and 31 rnds = 4"/10cm over two-color St st worked circularly using larger (3.5mm) needle. *Adjust the needle size as necessary to obtain correct gauge.*

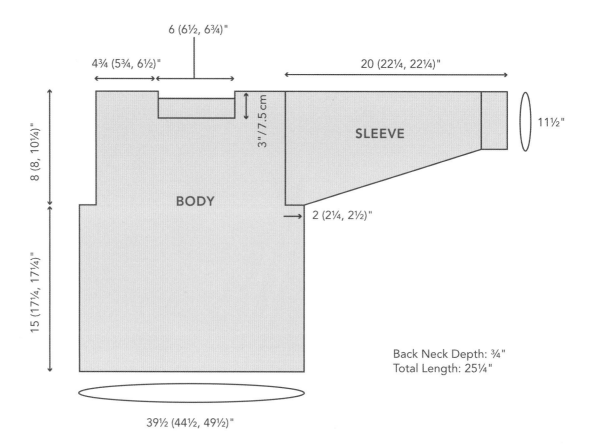

6 (6½, 6¾)"

4¾ (5¾, 6½)"

20 (22¼, 22¼)"

3"/7.5 cm

SLEEVE

11½"

8 (8, 10¼)"

BODY

2 (2¼, 2½)"

15 (17¼, 17¼)"

Back Neck Depth: ¾"
Total Length: 25¼"

39½ (44½, 49½)"

Construction Notes

1) This circularly knitted pullover with modified drop shoulders is worked as a tube up to the shoulder line by using steeks.

2) The shoulders are joined after sewing and cutting the armhole area.

3) The sleeves are knitted circularly from cuff to armhole, then sewn and cut to fit into the square-shaped armhole, and handsewn into the armholes. The neck stitches are then picked up for working the neckband.

4) A Twined Knitted technique is used for the edges.

5) Intarsia in the round is used for the little diamonds in the central panels (see chart A).

GLOSSARY

※ **steek** Stitches that are cast on, then later cut to create armholes or V-neck.

※ **sm** Slip marker

※ **Twined knitting** A technique used on the borders and neck edge. On the borders, one yarn remains in front and is purled, while the other yarn is held behind the work and stranded in the

back. Then the yarn behind the work is knitted while the yarn in front is stranded in the front. This creates a float of the B yarn on the front of the work. On the neck edge, both yarns are held in front and purled, with each yarn coming from underneath the yarn just worked; this creates a spiral effect.

※ **Intarsia in the round** Intarsia involves working one color back and forth (RS and WS) on a part of the design because that color is not used throughout the piece, but only in an isolated section. In this garment, the main structure is worked in the round, while the small diamonds in chart A (worked in B yarn) are worked in intarsia.

When working the diamonds, first cut off a one-yard (1m) length of B yarn. Work the first row of the diamond (one stitch), then weave the working end in a few stitches beyond that. For the next row, and future "WS" rows, the yarn will be on the far side of the small diamond. Work up to the stitches to be used for the diamond, slip the sts to be worked in this row for the little diamond, turn the work so the wrong side faces you, and purl the little diamond sts with the B yarn. Then, draw the end of the B yarn through a loop a few sts to the left away from the little diamond. Turn the work so the right side is again facing you.

3-needle bindoff Holding needles parallel with RS together and WS facing, k2tog from front and back needles, *k2tog from front and back needles and pass the first st over the second to bind off; rep from * to end.

INSTRUCTIONS FOR BORDER

With longer circular needle and A, CO 280 (320, 360) sts. Join, but don't twist sts on needle. Pm to indicate beg of rnd and sl marker every rnd. Work border chart beg where indicated as folls:

Border Pattern

(multiple of 20 sts)

Rnd 1 Join B, *p1 B, leave yarn in *front*, k1 A which remains in *back*, rep from * around.

Rnd 2 Bring B *forward*, *k1 A, p1 B in *front*; rep from * around.

Rnd 3 *K1 A, bring B *forward*, [k1 A, p1 B in *front*] 8 times, k1 A, take B to back of work, k2 A; rep from * around.

Rnd 4 *K2 A, bring B *forward*, [k1 A, p1 B in *front*] 7 times, k1 A, take B to *back* of work, k3 A; rep from * around.

Rnd 5 *K3 A, bring B *forward*, [k1 A, p1 B in *front*] 6 times, k1 A, take B to *back* of work, k3 A, k1 with B; rep from * around.

Rnd 6 *K1 B, k3 A, bring B *forward*, k1 A, p1 B in front] 5 times, k1 A, take B to *back* of work, k3 A, k1 B; rep from * around.

Rnd 7 *K2 B, k3 A, bring B *forward*, [k1 A, p1 B in *front*] 4 times, k1 A, take B to *back* of work, k3 A, k3 B; rep from * around.

Rnd 8 *K1 B, k5 A, bring B *forward*, [k1 A, p1 B in *front*] 3 times, k1 A, take B to *back* of work, k5 A, k2 B; rep from * around.

Rnd 9 *K7 A, bring B *forward*, [k1 A, p1 B in *front*] twice, k1 A, take B to *back* of work, k7 A, k1 B; rep from * around.

Rnd 10 *K8 A, bring B *forward*, k1 A, p1 B in A *front*, k1 A, take B to *back* of work, k9 A; rep from * around.

Rnd 11 Rep Rnd 1.

Rnd 12 Rep Rnd 2.

INSTRUCTIONS FOR THE BODY

The next round ensures that the center stitch of Chart A will be centered over a triangle of the twined knitted border in all four places of the garment as folls: the left underarm (as if you were wearing the garment), the front, the right underarm, and the back, in that order.

For size Small only

Next rnd With A, knit—280 sts.

For size Medium only

Next rnd With A, k79, k2tog, k77, k2tog, k78, k2tog, k31, k2tog, k47—316 sts.

For size Large only

Next rnd With A, k37, k2tog, k53, k2tog, k66, k2tog, k16, k2tog, k38, k2tog, k48, k2tog, k38, k2tog, k29, k2tog, k19—352 sts.

Pattern setup round

Rnd 1 *With A k1 (1, 4), pm, work chart A over 29 (31, 31) sts, pm, with A k1 (1, 4), work chart B over 11 (17, 17) sts, with A k1 (1, 5) sts, work Chart C over 27 sts, with A k1 (2, 4) sts, work Chart A over 29 (31, 31) sts, with A k1 (2, 4) sts, work Chart C over 27 sts, with A k1 (1, 5) sts, work Chart B over 11 (17, 17) sts; rep from * once more. (**Note:** Both the Charts A (underarm panels) are marked by a pair of stitch markers.)

Cont working all charts. Work the Base Rep of Chart A (Rnds 1–19) once and the Main Rep of Chart A (Rnds 20–37) 5 (5, 4) times, then work the Ending Rep of Chart A (Rnds 38–50) for the *underarm only* (the first and third locations of Chart A marked by the st markers), while cont to work main rep of Chart A on front and back.

Divide for armholes

Next rnd Work as established across garment, binding off sts at underarms as folls: k1 (1, 2), sm, BO 29 (31, 35) sts, sm, k111 (127, 141), sm, BO 29 (31, 35) sts, sm, k110 (126, 139).
(**Note:** The second marker of each pair at Chart A must be moved one stitch back. The last st to have a bound-off stitch pulled over it is not from the inside of the markers, but rather is included in the next group of sts.)

Setup steek K1 (1, 4), sm, CO 3 sts for steek, sm, work across to next marker, sm, CO 3 sts for steek, sm, work to end of rnd. Work even in pats

CHART A

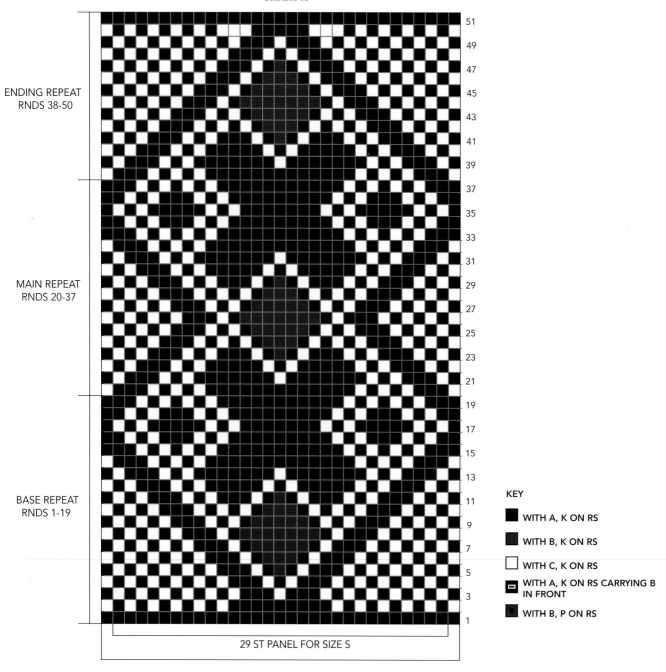

ENDING REPEAT
RNDS 38-50

MAIN REPEAT
RNDS 20-37

BASE REPEAT
RNDS 1-19

KEY

■ WITH A, K ON RS

■ WITH B, K ON RS

□ WITH C, K ON RS

▭ WITH A, K ON RS CARRYING B
IN FRONT

■ WITH B, P ON RS

29 ST PANEL FOR SIZE S

BORDER CHART

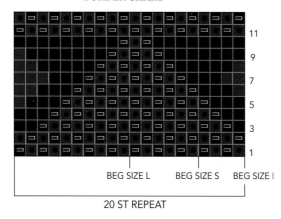

BEG SIZE L   BEG SIZE S   BEG SIZE I

20 ST REPEAT

CHART B (S only)

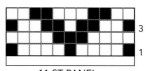

11 ST PANEL

CHART B (M AND L only)

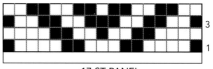

17 ST PANEL

as established, working the 3 steek sts *every* rnd as folls: p1 A, k1 B, p1 A. When a total of 7 Main Reps of Chart A have been worked on front and back, work the Ending Rep on the front *only*, while cont to work 1 more Main Rep on the back.

Front neck

Next rnd Work in pat across 39 (45, 52) sts, BO 41 (45, 47) sts, work 148 (170, 189) sts.

Setup steek Work in pat across 39 (45, 52) sts, pm, CO 3 sts, pm, work to end of rnd. Cont working in established pat, completing the 8th Main Rep of Chart A, then work Ending Rep of Chart A on the back.

Back neck

Next rnd Work in pat across 115 (133, 142) sts, BO 41 (45, 47) sts, work to end of rnd.

Setup steek Work in pat, CO 3 sts over back neck bindoff. Work in pat until the last rnd of Chart C has been worked. BO all steeks.

INSTRUCTIONS FOR SLEEVES

With size 2 (2, 4) dpns and A, CO 80 sts. Divide sts evenly between 3 needles. Join, taking care not to twist sts on needles. Pm to indicate beg of rnd and sl marker every rnd. Work Border chart, rep 4 times for 12 rnds. Cut C.

Next rnd With A, dec 5 sts evenly spaced around—75 sts.

Pattern setup rnd K1 A, pm, work Chart D over 7 (0, 0) sts, k2 A, work Chart B over 11 (17, 17) sts, k2 A, work Chart A over 29 (31, 31) sts, k2 A, work Chart B over 11 (17, 17) sts, k2 A, work Chart D over 7 (0, 0) sts, pm, k1 A. Work even in pats as established for 5 rnds.

Next (inc) rnd Inc 1 st after first marker and 1 st before 2nd marker. Cont to inc while maintaining established pat as folls:

For size Small only

Inc every 6th rnd 3 times, then every 7th rnd 14 times—111 sts.

For size Medium only

Inc every 7th rnd 10 times, then every 8th rnd 7 times—111 sts.

For size Large only

Inc every 4th rnd 22 times, then every 5th rnd 10 times-141 sts.

CHART C

60 RND REPEAT

61 59 57 55 53 51 49 47 45 43 41 39 37 35 33 31 29 27 25 23 21 19 17 15 13 11 9 7 5 3 1

27 ST PANEL

CHART D

2 ST PANEL

KEY

■ WITH A, K ON RS
□ WITH C, K ON RS

When incs are completed, work even, beg the Ending Rep of Chart A when appropriate. Then, with A only, purl for 1"/2.5cm for a sleeve facing. BO loosely, leaving a 1 yd/1m long tail for sewing down the facing later.

FINISHING

Block pieces before assembling; this will aid in keeping the sts in place once the steeks are cut.

Armholes

Machine stitch two lines of stitching on either side of the center steek stitch. Cut the armholes open by cutting up the middle of the central steek st. With RS tog, join the shoulders using 3-needle bindoff.

Sleeves

Machine stitch two lines the length of the body underam bindoff on either side of the 2-st line of A; cut down the middle of the A line. Handsew the sleeves into the armholes, then sew down the facings (with yarn tail) to the inside of the body, hiding the raw edges of the machine stitching and cutting.

Neckband

Machine stitch two lines of stitching to either side of the center steek stitch for both the front neck steek and the back neck steek. Cut the two neck steeks.

Twined neckband

Join A at back right neck, pick up and k 41 (45, 47) sts across back, 1 st in corner, 28 sts along side of neck, 1 st in corner, 41 (45, 47) sts across front, 1 st in corner, 28 sts along side of neck, 1 st in corner—142 (150, 154) sts. Join and pm to indicate beg of rnd and sl marker every rnd. Work rnds according to directions *below*, AT THE SAME TIME, work each corner as a double decrease, with the corner st being the second of the two slipped sts as folls: slip 2 sts tog k-wise, k1 with A, p2sso.

Rnd 1 Join B. With both yarns held in *front* for the entire rnd and bringing new yarn from underneath the just-used yarn, *p1 A, p1 B; rep from * around. (**Note:** The yarns will spiral around each other.)
Rnd 2 Knit with A.
Rnd 3 Purl with A.
Rnd 4 Rep Rnd 1. BO k-wise using A. With a tapestry needle, weave in loose yarn tails to the WS of work and secure.

No longer considered undesirable, black merino sheep like this one produce some of the finest and softest wools with naturally rich colors.

MOREHOUSE FARM

LOCATED IN THE HUDSON RIVER VALLEY IN NEW YORK STATE, MOREHOUSE FARM WAS STARTED

after Albrecht Pichler and his wife, Margrit Lohrer, purchased a champion merino sheep flock at the National Merino Show in Harrisburg, Pennsylvania. Their goal had been to grow the finest wool in the United States and to reintroduce merino sheep to the northeastern corner of the United States.

Merino wool has long been esteemed as the premier wool. Merino sheep originated in Spain and they have set the standard for other breeds of sheep, which are commonly rated by how much merino blood they have. Fleeces of merino sheep are very soft and fine, with a long staple length. Although merino fleece was once a wool grower's pride and joy, this breed of sheep had all but disappeared on the east coast of the United States. With the popularity of synthetic fibers and sinking wool prices, the fine-wooled sheep were

falling out of favor with the farmers.

The early '80s brought a renewed interest in all things natural, and pure merino wool became the industry standard for luxurious wool garments. In 1987, Albrecht and Margrit imported the first two superfine Merino rams from Australia into the United States. These superfine merino are bred in Australia and New Zealand for their superior fine wool.

Today, as part of their discerning breeding program, Albrecht and Margrit test and retest the wool to make sure the progeny has the characteristics that they continue to look for. Not only do they want very strong fine fibers, but they want long fibers as well. They also want their sheep to have fleeces that are brilliantly white and dense or, intensely black, depending on the particular sheep's coloring and the desired yarn color.

Albrecht and Margrit continue to sell their rams across the United States and are revered as producers of some of the loveliest merino wool around, frequently winning awards for the quality of their sheep. They have also begun raising black merino sheep and they blend in varying amounts of the black to create a wide range of "natural" colors. In the past few years, they also have dyed their yarns.

They showcase their unspun wool, a line of yarn, patterns, and finished knitted and woven goods at their lovely, airy store called Sheep's Clothing in Milan, New York, near their farm. In addition, Albrecht and Margrit can frequently be found at sheep and wool events. Morehouse Farm also sells its yarns and patterns at the greenmarkets in New York City. (Visit their website at morehousefarm.com to see what Albrecht and Margrit are up to!)

Back Home in Vermont Sweater

DESIGNED BY MARJORIE MOUREAU

For this top-down sweater, Marj chose Green Mountain Spinnery's wonderful organic yarn. The yarn has a crisp edge and readily shows off cables and other patterning. Only four rows are needed to create the simple but effective "Twists and Ribs" pattern stitch used in this classic sweater pattern for men and women. The pattern repeats are perfect for those who are frequently interrupted, but the best part about this pattern is that there is very little seaming at the end.

Skill Level
Intermediate

Sizes
Instructions are for Small. Changes for Medium and Large are in parenthesis. Shown in Size Large.

Finished Measurements
Bust: 39 (44, 48¾)"/99 (112, 124)cm
Length: 23 (24.5, 26)"/58.5 (62.25, 66)cm

Yarn
VERMONT ORGANIC by Green Mountain Spinnery, 4oz/113g skeins, each aprox 250yds/229m (100% organic wool) or a medium weight yarn

• 7 (8,8) skeins Gray

Needles & Notions
• Sizes 4 and 5 (3.5 and 3.75mm) circular needles 24 and 29"/60cm and 74cm long or *size needed to obtain gauge*

• Waste yarn

• Spare circular needles

• Stitch markers

• Tapestry needle

Gauge
23 sts and 27 rows = 4"/10cm over Twists and Ribs pat (blocked) using larger needles. *Adjust the needle size if necessary to obtain the correct gauge.*

Construction Notes

1) This saddle-shoulder pullover is worked from the top down, beginning with the saddles, front and back necks and yokes.

2) The sleeves are picked up from the armhole and worked back and forth to cuff.

3) The front and back are joined and worked in the round down to bottom ribbing.

4) The turtleneck is worked last.

5) Work all incs and decs inside selvedge sts.

6) When increasing on saddle, underarm, and sleeve, use "k1 in front and back of st" inc.

GLOSSARY

RT Knit the next two sts together and leave on left-hand needle; insert right hand needle between these two sts and knit the first st again; slip both sts from needle.

Twists and Ribs

Worked back and forth (multiple of 7 sts plus 3)
Row 1 (RS) K1 (selvedge), *k1, p2, k2, p2; rep from * to last 2 sts, k1; k1 (selvedge).

Row 2 P1 (selv), *p1, k2, p2, k2; rep from * to last 2 sts, p1; p1 (selv).

Row 3 K1 (selv), *k1, p2, RT, p2; rep from * to last 2 sts, k1, k1 (selv).

Row 4 Same as Row 2.

Rep these 4 rows for Tiwst and Ribs pat.

Worked in the round (multiple of 7 sts)

Rnds 1, 2, and 4: *P1, k1, p2, k2, p1; rep from * around.

Rnd 3: *P1, k1, p2, RT, p1; rep from * around.

Rep Rnds 1-4 for Twists and Ribs pat.

INSTRUCTIONS FOR THE SWEATER

Saddles (make two)

With larger needle, CO 24 sts. Work in Twists and Ribs pat for 28 (32, 36) rows; cut yarn and place sts on waste yarn to be worked later.

Front

Left Front Neck Hold one saddle piece with RS facing and sts on waste yarn to the *left*. Using

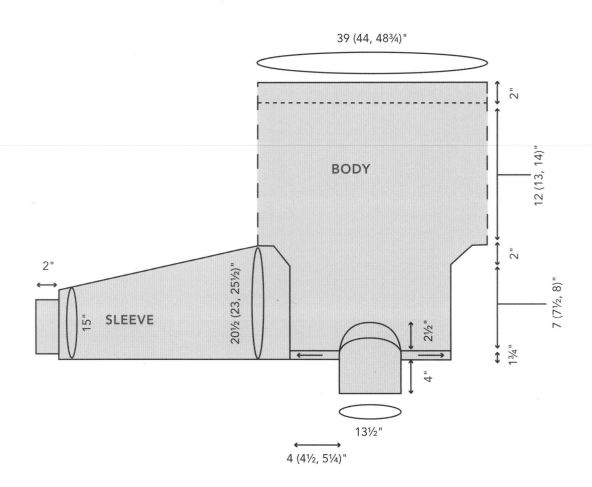

39 (44, 48¾)"

2"

BODY

12 (13, 14)"

2"

2½"

7 (7½, 8)"

1¾"

2"

SLEEVE

15"

20½ (23, 25½)"

4"

13½"

4 (4½, 5¼)"

larger needle, pick up and k15 (17,19) sts evenly along one selvedge edge.

Next row Knit, inc 9 (14, 19) sts evenly across—24 (31, 38) sts.

Next 6 rows Work Twists and Ribs pat, beg with Row 3.

Neck Shaping

Inc row (RS) K1 (selv), M1, work in pat to end of row. Rep Inc row every RS row 5 more times, working new sts into pat—30 (37, 44) sts. Cut yarn and slip sts onto a spare needle.

Right Front Neck Work as for left front neck *except* hold saddle with the sts on waste yarn to the *right* and reverse neck shaping by working M1 at the *end* of every RS row 6 times. Do not cut yarn.

Front yoke

Join neck

Next Row Work across right front sts in pat as established; CO 27 sts for the center front neck; work across left front sts on spare needle—87 (101, 115) sts. Work even in pat until piece measures 7 (7½, 8)"/18 (19, 20)cm from saddles, end with Row 4.

Armhole Shaping Inc 1 at beg of next 14 rows, working new sts into pattern—101 (115, 129) sts. Cut yarn and place sts on waste yarn.

Back

Back Neck With RS of right saddle facing and using larger needle, pick up and k15 (17, 19) sts evenly along opposite selvedge edge.

Next row Knit and inc 9 (14, 19) sts evenly across row—24 (31, 38) sts. Work Rows 3 and 4 of pat. Cut yarn and slip sts onto spare needle. Rep on left saddle, but do not cut yarn.

Join neck: Work across left shoulder in pat as established, CO 39 sts for back neck, work across right shoulder sts on spare needle—87 (101, 115) sts. Work as for front yoke through armhole shaping—101 (115, 129) sts.

Sleeves

Slip saddle sts from waste yarn to spare needle. With RS facing, larger needle and starting on front yoke, pick up and k35 (42, 49) sts evenly along *straight edge* of yoke; work the 24 sts on spare needle in pat as established, then pick up and k35 (42, 49) sts evenly along *straight edge* of back

TWISTS AND RIBS

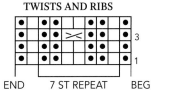

END   7 ST REPEAT   BEG

KEY

☐ K ON RS, P ON WS

▣ P ON RS, K ON WS

⋈ RT

yoke—94 (108, 122) sts. *Do not pick up sts in 14 angled rows.* Work in pat as established and inc 1 at beg of next 14 rows, working new sts into pat—108 (122, 136) sts.

Underarm CO 5 sts at beg of the next 2 rows, knit them on the RS and purl them on the WS—118 (132, 146) sts. Work 3 rows even.

Dec row (RS) K1, k2tog, work in pat as established to last 3 sts, ssk, k1. Rep Dec row every 8th row 4 (0, 0) times, every 6th row 11 (9, 0) times, then every 4th row 0 (13, 29) times—86 sts. Work even until sleeve measures 17 (18, 19)"/43 (46, 48)cm or desired length from the underarm sts, end with Row 4. Change to smaller needle.

Cuff

Next Row (RS) Work across row, knitting tog the 2 sts of RT.

Next row K2tog each pair of knit sts to obtain k1, p1 ribbing plus a selvedge st at each edge. Work in ribbing for 2"/5cm. BO lossely in rib.

Body

Slip front and back yoke sts from waste yarn onto larger 29" needle. With RS facing and beg at edge of Front yoke, attach yarn and work across in pat as established. CO 11 sts at end of row for underarm, work across back yoke, CO 11 sts—224 (252, 280) sts. PM and join. Work Twists and Ribs pat in the round until body measures 12 (13, 14)"/30.5 (33, 35.5)cm from underarm sts, end after Row 4. Change to smaller 29" needle.

Ribbing

Next rnd Work around, knitting tog the 2 sts for RT—192 (216, 240)sts rem. Work in k1, p2 ribbing for 2"/5cm. BO loosely in rib.

Turtleneck

(Designer Tip: For a neat transition, pick up one st for each twist and one st for each pair of purl sts along straight edges of neck, then try to align the knit and purl sts of collar ribbing with the knit and purl sts of body.)

With smaller 24" needle, pick up and k28 sts along back neck, 14 sts along left shoulder, 38 sts along front neck and 14 sts along right shoulder—94 sts. PM and join. Work in k1, p1 ribbing for 4"/10 cm. BO very loosely in rib.

FINISHING

Sew tog the underarm yoke sts and corresponding sleeve sts. Sew sleeve seams. With a tapestry needle, weave in loose tails to WS and secure. Block to measurements.

Sheep

Goat

What is the difference between sheep and goats?

Genetically, sheep and goats are different, but a simple way to tell the difference between the two animals is to look at their tails. Goats' tails go up unless they are scared, sick, or distressed. Sheeps' tails hang down. Sheep tend to graze, eating grass and clover close to the ground, almost to dirt level. Goats are browsers and prefer to eat leaves, vines, and twigs. They are agile and will stand on their hind legs to sample something appealing. In fact, goats are being used to eliminate noxious weeds, such as leafy spurge, from fields in the plains, and their waste acts as a natural herbicide.

ABOUT GREEN MOUNTAIN SPINNERY

THE GOALS OF GREEN MOUNTAIN SPINNERY ARE TO HELP SUSTAIN REGIONAL SHEEP FARMING, to create the highest quality yarns, and to develop environmentally sound ways to process natural fibers. Established in 1981, the spinnery creates yarns for retail and wholesale and offers a gallery of more than 50 Vermont designer patterns to support its yarns. It also spins customized yarns for individuals who raise their own natural fibers. The owners are David Ritchie, Claire Wilson, and Libby Mills.

Green Mountain Spinnery has been at the forefront of producing yarn in an environmentally responsible manner. This includes its proprietary "greenspun" processing, which uses no chemicals in the cleaning and processing oils. When the fleece arrives, it is full of grease, dirt, and lanolin. The scouring and scrubbing department removes it with vegetable-based—not petroleum-based—soaps.

Next the fleece goes through the picker, which lines up the fibers, opening them and making them fluffier. A picker is a crude "organizer."

If this is not done, the fibers will be so dense, they will be difficult to spin.

At this point in any milling process, some moisture needs to be put back into the fiber. This could be petroleum-based or as this eco-friendly mill prefers, greenspun. Green Mountain Spinnery uses a soap mixed with certified-organic canola oil, which is sprinkled over the fiber with compressed air streams.

The spinnery now has evolved into producing organic yarn, moving forward into fairly uncharted territory. The Organic Trade Association is still mapping out the requirements in the organic fiber industry. The association maintains that keeping petroleum out of the washing and spinning steps is important. Also, it has found that there should be no residues of herbicides or pesticides in organic yarn.

Despite some real challenges when it comes to raising sheep organically, the Green Mountain Spinnery has been raising its sheep organically since 1998, even

before the national organic certification kicked in, using the certification guidelines of NOFA (Northeast Organic Farmers Association).

Green Mountain Spinnery is earnest in its endeavor to do the best it can "to remain true to our organic selves," as David Ritchie says. It wants to buy locally as well. All the fibers it uses—alpaca, mohair, wool, and organic cotton—are grown in the United States and purchased directly from individual growers, whenever possible.

From the initial contact with the fiber grower through the final labeling and approval of each finished skein of yarn, the spinnery pays careful attention to every step and detail in the yarn-making process. The yarns are created on-site with vintage equipment. The dynamic capabilities of this venerable machinery is matched with a keen understanding of the nuances of the original fiber blends. Throughout the entire process, the inherent liveliness of the natural fibers is respected.

Here & There—Stone's Sweater

DESIGNED BY MARGARET KLEIN WILSON

This is the sweater I wish I had had as a child to yank on in those seasons between seasons instead of a winter coat. Brisk fall afternoons and warming spring days always drew me out of doors—here and there. The generous neck makes this sweater ideal for slipping over lighter layers of clothing. A mock seam in both body and sleeves gives this generously sized pullover tunic the stretch, ease, and comfort necessary for getting into the spirit of jumping in leaf piles, tree climbing, and other seasonal recreations. The Vandyke check pattern infuses the sweater with energy and a sense of motion. Sage and Wedgewood reflect the moody blues and pine greens of a late October afternoon. These same tones reappear in spring looking fresh and energetic in late afternoon blue skies and the luminous greens of emerging foliage.

Skill Level
Intermediate

Sizes
Instructions are for children's size 4–6. Changes for 8–10 and 12–14 are in parentheses. Shown in size 12–14.

Finished Measurements
Chest 26 (32, 39)"/66 (81, 99)cm
Length 15 (19, 23)"/38 (48, 58.5)cm

Yarn
MOSTLY MERINO WORSTED WEIGHT, 2oz/56.75g skeins, each approx 125yd/114m (77% merino wool/23% kid mohair) or a medium weight yarn
• 4 (6, 7) skeins in Wedgewood Blue (MC)
• 1 (1, 1) skein in Sage (CC)

Needles & Notions
• Sizes 7 and 8 (4.5 and 5mm) circular needles, 24"/60cm or 29"/73.5cm long *or size needed to obtain gauge*
• One set (4) each sizes 7 and 8 (4.5 and 5mm) double-pointed needles (dpns)
• Stitch holders
• Stitch markers
• Tapestry needle

Gauge
16 sts and 22 rnds = 4"/10cm over St st using larger needle.
16 sts and 22 rows = 4"/10cm over Vandyke Check pat using smaller needle.
Adjust the needle sizes as necessary to obtain correct gauge.

Construction Notes

1) The body of this pullover is worked in the round from the bottom up.

2) It is then divided into back and front at the underarm and worked back and forth to the shoulders.

3) Shoulders are joined using a 3-needle bindoff. By working this bindoff with the wrong sides together, you will create a ridge that nearly mirrors the back and front shoulder welts.

4) The sleeves are worked in the round from the armhole down.

5) There are no seams to sew.

GLOSSARY

▨ **3-needle bindoff** Holding needles parallel with WS together and RS facing, k2tog from front and back needles, *k2tog from front and back needles and pass the first st over the second to bind off; rep from * to end.

▨ **Welt Pattern A** (worked in the round)
Rnds 1 and 2 Purl with MC.
Rnd 3 Knit with CC.
Rnd 4 Knit with MC.

▨ **Welt Pattern B** (worked back and forth)
Row 1 (RS) Purl with MC.
Row 2 Knit with MC.
Row 3 Knit with CC.
Row 4 Purl with MC.

▨ **Vandyke Check pattern** (multiple of 8 sts)
Row 1 (RS) Knit.
Row 2 *K4, p4; rep from * to end.
Row 3 *P1, k4, p3; rep from * to end.
Row 4 *K2, p4, k2; rep from * to end.
Row 5 *P3, k4, p1; rep from * to end.
Row 6 *P4, k4; rep from * to end.
Row 7 Knit.
Rows 8–11 *K4, p4; rep from * to end.
Row 12 Purl.
Row 13 *P4, k4; rep from * to end.
Row 14 *K1, p4, k3; rep from * to end.
Row 15 *P2, k4, p2; rep from * to end.
Row 16 *K3, p4, k1; rep from * to end.
Row 17 *K4, p4; rep from * to end.
Row 18 Purl.
Rows 19–22 *P4, k4; rep from* to end.
Rep Rows 1–22 for Vandyke Check pat.

VANDYKE CHECK PATTERN

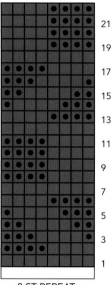

8 ST REPEAT

KEY

■ WITH MC, K ON RS, P ON WS

▨ WITH MC, P ON RS, K ON WS

□ WITH CC, K ON RS, P ON WS

WELT PATTERN

4 ST REPEAT

MOSTLY MERINO

MARGARET KLEIN WILSON IS THE OWNER OF MOSTLY MERINO, A FIBER STUDIO SPECIALIZING IN

hand-dyed luxury merino and mohair knitting yarns, patterns, and knitting kits since 1990. With her family, she moved from suburban Boston to a hillside farm in southern Vermont in 1988, and acquired a few Merino sheep to keep the farm fields open. A year and three bags of wool later, Mostly Merino was born.

A self-taught shepherd, dyer, and designer, Margaret finds inspiration as much in the process and collaborative nature of bringing wool to market as she does in the satisfaction of keeping sheep. Each stage of having her yarns produced is one of affection, attention, nuance, and

craftsmanship. The stages include maintaining a flock of sheep, acquiring additional fine wool and mohair fiber from regional farms, having these spun locally, and then over-dyeing the skeins in small dye lots.

Margaret recognizes the value of each stage: "I appreciate that all the materials are shepherded from one process to the next so intentionally, from hands to hands to hands. Throughout, these premium fibers remain lively and energetic. The finished yarn is soft, elastic, and full of character. And then the yarn finds its way to the knitter, who gives it another life. Amazing."

The knitter who purchases mostly Merino is an important part of every process. As Margaret says, "The simple act of purchasing locally produced yarns has an immediate economic impact. It supports the infrastructure necessary to sustain a lively, local agricultural community: a veterinarian, a feed store, farms that grow hay, a spinnery, a regional sheep festival. Knitters not only have the pleasure of working with exceptional one-of-a-kind yarns, but they also know they are contributing to sustaining a way of life—truly patrons of the arts and agriculture. Everybody wins."

INSTRUCTIONS FOR THE SWEATER

Body

With smaller needle and MC, CO 104 (128, 156) sts. Join, taking care not to twist sts on needle. Pm to indicate beg of rnd and sl marker every rnd. Work Rnds 1–4 of Welt Pat A twice. Change to larger needle and St st (k every rnd).
Next and all foll rnds Incorporate a p2 mock side seam as folls: *p1, k 50 (62, 76) sts, p1; rep from * around. Rep last rnd until body measures 10 (12 15)"/25.5 (30.5, 38)cm from beg. Work Rnds 1–4 of Welt Pat A once. Change to smaller needle.

Divide for armholes

Next rnd *K2 (4, 6), pm, work Row 1 of Vandyke Check pat across next 48 (56, 64) sts, pm, k2 (4, 6); rep from * once more. Place first 52 (64, 78) sts on holder for front.

Back

Next row Knit to marker, work Row 2 of Vandyke Check pat to next marker, knit to end. Cont working garter st edges and Vandyke Check pat between markers as folls:
For size Small only
Work Rows 3–22.
For size Medium only
Work Rows 3–22, then Rows 1–7.
For size Large only
Work Rows 3–22, then Rows 1–17. The armhole should measure approx 4 (5½, 6)"/10 (14, 15)cm. Change to larger needle. Work 2 (2, 3) reps of Welt Pat B, dropping markers on first row.

Back neck shaping

Next row (RS) K12 (17, 22) for right back shoulder, BO center 28 (30, 34) sts for back neck and k12 (17, 22) rem sts for left back shoulder. Place shoulder sts onto separate holders.

Front

Place 52 (64, 78) sts from front holder onto smaller needle. Work garter st edges and Vandyke Check

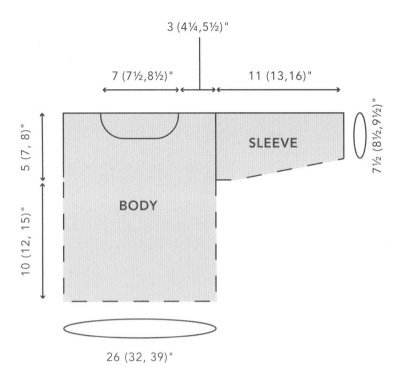

pat as for back. Change to larger needle. Work 2 rows of Welt Pat B, dropping markers on first row.

Front neck shaping

Next row (RS) Cont in pat as established, work across first 16 (21, 27) sts, join 2nd ball of yarn, BO center 20 (22, 22) sts for front neck, work across rem 16 (21, 27) sts. Work next row even. **Dec row (RS)** Work Welt Pat B to 3 sts before neck, k2tog, k1; with 2nd ball of yarn, k1, ssk, work Welt Pat B to end. Rep Dec row every RS row 3 (3, 4) times more—12 (17, 22) sts each side. Work even until front measures same length as back to shoulder, end with a WS row. With MC, work 2 rows in St st. Place shoulder sts onto separate holders. With WS tog, join front and back shoulders using 3-needle bindoff. Weave in all yarn ends.

Sleeves

With RS facing, larger dpns and MC, beg at underarm and pick up and k23 (27, 30) sts evenly spaced to shoulder, then pick up and k23 (27, 30) sts evenly spaced to underarm—46 (54, 60) sts. Join and pm to indicate beg of rnd and sl marker every rnd. Work in St st, purling the first and last st of each rnd to create a mock underarm seam as for body. Work even for 1½ (2, 2)"/4 (5, 5)cm. **Dec rnd** P1, ssk, knit last 4 sts, k2tog, k1, p1. Rep dec rnd every 6th rnd 6 (7, 8) times more—32 (38, 42) sts. Work even until the sleeve measures approx 9 (11, 14)"/23 (28, 35.5)cm or 2"/5cm shorter than desired length.

Next rnd Knit, dec 2 (4, 4) sts evenly spaced around—30 (34, 38) sts. Change to smaller dpns. Work Rows 1–4 of Welt Pat A twice, then Rows 1 and 2 once. BO all sts loosely k-wise.

FINISHING

Neckband

With RS facing, and smaller dpns, MC pick up and k7 (9, 11) sts along left front neck, 20 (22, 22) sts along front neck, 7 (9, 11) sts along right front neck, pm, then 28 (30, 34) sts along back neck, pm— approx 62 (70, 78) sts. Purl next 3 rnds. **Last rnd** *Purl to 3 sts before marker, p2tog, p1, sm, p1, p2tog; rep from * once more. BO all sts loosely p-wise. With a tapestry needle, weave in loose yarn tails to the WS of work and secure. Wet-block to measurements.

THIRTEEN MILE LAMB & WOOL COMPANY

COMMITTED TO BEING "PREDATOR FRIENDLY," THIRTEEN MILE LAMB & WOOL COMPANY, OF BELGRADE,

Montana, is owned and operated by Becky Weed (a geologist by training) and Dave Tyler (an engineer). Neither of them grew up in ranch or farm families, so they have learned much since they started the farm in 1987.

Becky feels that "sometimes our late arrival to agriculture is as much help as hindrance. As a geologist and an engineer, both of us have had professional careers that have given us the chance to see landscape in a context that includes, but is not limited to, agriculture. That has made it seem natural to ask hard questions about what the goals of a modern ranch should be." The couple is dedicated to sustainable agriculture.

At Thirteen Mile Farm, Becky and David raise sheep without using chemical fertilizers and herbicides on the fields. The sheep eat grass, clover, and alfalfa, and a little organic barley. No antibiotics or hormone supplements are used; their lambs are certified organic by the Montana State Department of Agriculture.

Their livestock is fenced out of the creeks to protect both the local wildlife habitat and the quality of the sheep's drinking water. Their principal protection against native predators are guard llamas and their own vigilance. Because they have made a formal commitment not to use lethal control methods against native species, such as coyotes, bears, wolves, and mountain lions, their ranch is certified as "predator friendly." It is a choice they have made, like many of their land management decisions, acknowledging the risk in the interest of learning how to coexist with native species while caring for the land.

Their wool blends are spun by Green Mountain Spinnery in Vermont (see page 53), because Becky and David are willing and able to create the unique variegated yarn blends and because they use non–petroleum-based soaps to prepare the raw wool for spinning.

In addition to offering yarn, Thirteen Mile Lamb & Wool Company sells fleeces, blankets, buttons made from old juniper wood fence posts scavenged on Becky and David's homestead, sheepskins, and lamb. You can check out the company's latest and extensive offerings anytime at lambandwool.com.

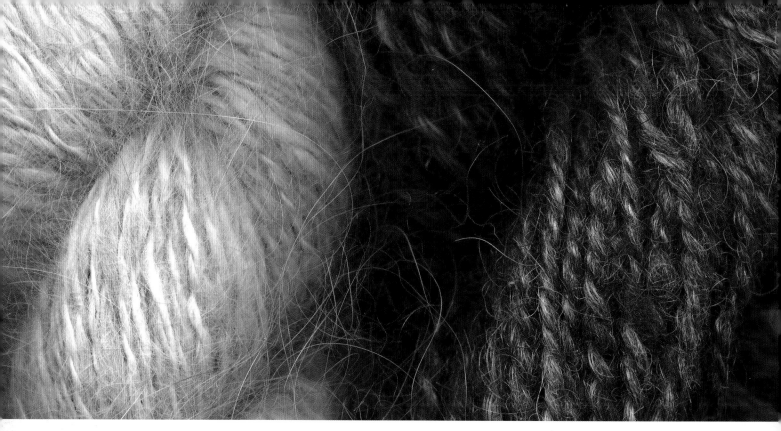

Chapter 2

CAMELIDS, GOATS, BUNNIES, OTHER FIBER-BEARING BEASTIES AND SILK

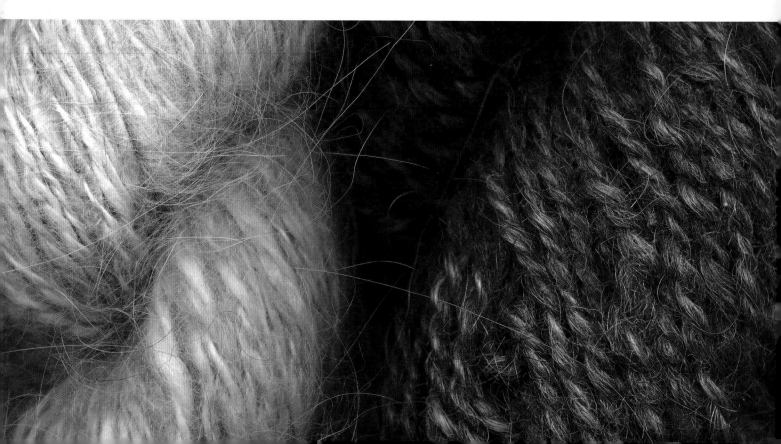

Warmth and protection are not the only aspects of clothing that humans care about. There is also a craving for fabrics that are soft. In addition, there is the emotional and exclusive appeal of anything that is exotic or imported. Of course, a garment should be pleasing to the eye, too. No doubt, even the early cavemen pushed on and hunted just a little bit farther away in order to get the choicest skins. This love affair with out-of-the-ordinary fibers persists today, and knitters want the chance to knit with all of them whether they are cashmere, qiviut, yak, camel, or angora.

Opposite
Camels (shown), llamas, alpacas, guanacos, vicunas—all are members of the camelid family; their undercoats are highly valued.

Many fiber-bearing animals around the world have a common trait: they grow a double coat of hair. The coarse outer coat (guard hair) protects the animals from the harsh environment and keeps out debris and moisture. The undercoat (also called down), insulates the animal from temperature extremes. This down tends to be lightweight, soft, and very warm. Obtaining the down and separating it from the coarse outer coat can be fairly labor-intensive, but once you experience the softness and warmth of these fibers, you will find it is worth the effort.

After the animals are rounded up, the down is either combed off or the fleece is sheared. Experienced sorters then carefully remove the coarse hairs, and the soft down is used to spin yarn.

In this chapter, we will take a look at some of the other animals besides sheep that provide fiber that can be turned into luxurious yarn. In addition to using the fiber from some of the better-known fiber-bearing animals such as alpacas, llamas, angora goats, and angora bunnies, several producers are turning fibers from dogs, fox, and even the brushings from chinchillas into yarn to tantalize the most adventuresome knitters. And

silk, produced from the cocoon of the silkworm, will also be covered, along with the ancient art of sericulture—the process of breeding moths to produce silk.

Camelids

Personable faces with soft eyes surrounded by curly eyelashes make camelids (camels) difficult to resist. Members of the biological family of *Camelidae* produce some lovely fibers. Today there are three basic species left:
1) Dromedary camels (one hump) of the Arabian desert
2) Bactrian camels (two humps) of Asia
3) The camelids of South America, which include llamas, guanaco, alpaca, vicuna, and paco-vicuna (a new North American strain of the South American llamas)

About 40 to 50 million years ago, the camelid family originated and evolved on the central plains of North America. About 3 million years ago, their descendants migrated to Asia and northern Africa, evolving into camels. They also migrated to South America, where they evolved into the llama-related species. Coming in many shapes and sizes, all camelids are similar in genetic makeup and can be cross-bred with each other and produce fertile offspring. Because they evolved in a semidesert environment, they have adapted to cope with heat and dehydration.

CAMELS

Camels were domesticated thousands of years ago and they became the main sources of transportation, shade, milk, meat, fiber, and hides for desert inhabitants. Today, in more modernized areas where their services are no longer used for transportation, camels are valued as racing animals. However, in many parts of Africa and Asia, camels still turn water wheels, pull ploughs, and transport people and goods along paths that can't accommodate wheeled vehicles.

Camels can range in color from cream to almost black. They molt in the spring and grow a new coat by the autumn. They also have two kinds of coats—a soft downy undercoat and a courser top coat. Camels can shed as much as 5 pounds of hair each time they molt! Their long coarse outer fibers have been felted and used by the Mongolians to make yurts (felted, tentlike structures that protect against the elements). Also, camel fiber has long held an acclaimed role in the world of fashion. Today, knitters look for the yarn made from the down of the camels to turn into soft and wonderful yarn. Their hair is also used to make fine-quality paintbrushes.

Camel Truths

Camels tend to be good-tempered, patient, and intelligent. The grunts and noises they make when they stand up sound like the heavy breathing of someone who is exercising.

Camels have leathery feet with two toes on each foot. When a camel walks, its feet flatten out so the animal doesn't sink into the sand. Unlike many animals, camels move both feet on one side and then both feet on the other side to walk. This rolling gait, which is similar to the rolling motion of a boat, gives camels the nickname Ship of the Desert!

The camel does not store water in its hump, which is a mound of fatty tissue used for energy. If the reserved energy is used, the mound becomes flabby and shrinks. If the camel draws in too much fat, the small remaining lump will flop over from its upright position. Camels need very little water if their regular diet contains good, moisture-rich pasture. However, these animals can drink a huge amount of water—21 gallons in ten minutes—and their system allows them to preserve water very efficiently.

LLAMAS

One look into the soft warm eyes of a llama, with its charming quizzical expression, and the allure of this usually gentle animal is clear—it has even become a popular pet. A part of the extended camel family, llamas produce a fiber that is long and fine. The fiber is hollow, trapping air and making it warmer than wool of the same weight. Llamas have two coats: an outer layer of coarser guard top hairs that repel moisture and a finer undercoat that provides warmth. Llama fiber ranges greatly. Baby llamas can have fiber as soft as baby alpacas—about 20 microns—but usually their fiber is more than 30 microns.

In addition to providing a luxurious fiber, llamas are kept as pets and pack animals. Like other camelids, llamas have soft padded feet with two toes and when they walk along a trail, they are very gentle to the environment.

Llamas are also used for guarding sheep. Margaret Klein Wilson, proprietor of Mostly Merino (see her design on page 54), has a guard llama named Mac. One day when she went out to the pasture, Mac was persistently humming (llamas communicate by humming). She didn't pay a lot of attention, but the next day, he was even more emphatic with his humming. Margaret followed Mac and he led her to a coyote he had trampled, perhaps just to let her know that he had been doing his job.

The llamas' guarding skill was discovered by accident. Llamas were introduced into North America in the 1800s and 1900s when zoos and private animal collectors brought llamas to the United States. As more llamas came, they were occasionally pastured with sheep, and their owners noticed that fewer sheep were being lost to predation. Rather than use aggressive methods such as guns and traps to be predator free, some who raise sheep use llamas to protect their flocks.

A part of the extended camel family, llamas produce fibers in a range of natural shades. Like the alpaca, they produce a hollow fiber, making it warmer than wool of the same weight.

Opposite
Who can resist the gentle demeanor, inquisitive manner, and intelligence of a llama? This amenable camelid not only makes the perfect buddy, but also produces hollow fiber that is warmer than wool.

> Llamas have two coats—the coarser outer layer's top hairs repel moisture and the finer undercoat provides warmth. Their fiber spans a wide range. Baby llamas can have fiber as soft as baby alpacas at about 20 microns, but usually their fiber is over 30 microns. Llamas weigh 250 to 500 pounds (113.5–227kg).

PEACE FLEECE

PEACE FLEECE WAS STARTED BY PETER HAGERTY AND HIS WIFE, MARTY TRACY, TO HELP HISTORIC political enemies cooperate and prosper through trade: tending livestock, knitting, and needlework were the common bonds that brought the discordant peoples together! For instance, Peace Fleece offers knitting yarn made from a blend of Israeli and Palestinian wool. Additionally, the company sells supplies for felting and spinning, numerous kits, lush hand-dyed yarns, charming hand-painted knitting needles, and wooden buttons. Check out www.peacefleece.com for moving stories of Peter and Marty's adventures as well as descriptions of their products. As Peace Fleece demonstrates, knitters and shepherds can take a hands-on role in the efforts of world peace!

Girls' Night Out Sweater and Hat

DESIGNED BY KATHY ZIMMERMAN

Kathy Zimmerman rules when it comes to creating cozy warm pullovers with lots of texture! She added a snuggly hat to go with this sweater. Made in a more masculine color, this hat and sweater set would be great for a guy as well.

Kathy named this sweater in honor of her monthly get-together with friends. She goes out to dinner and a movie—typically watching a chick flick that doesn't interest the husbands—with her friends Karen, Darlene, and sometimes a few others. Kathy came up with this sweater as the perfect choice for what she would want to wear all evening long, whether they choose the local retro diner, pub grub fare, Chinese, or Italian followed by a movie or videos at Karen's house.

Kathy opted for Classic Elite Montera. She says, "This llama wool blend is my all-time favorite yarn, perfect for our chilly Pennsylvania winters (we are in ski country, and this sweater will do double duty après-ski, too)." Kathy believes sweaters are "knitted hugs" and this is certainly a great hug to knit for yourself or someone you care about!

Skill Level
Intermediate

Sizes

Sweater
Instructions are for Small. Changes for Medium, Large, and X-Large are in parentheses. Shown in size Medium.

Hat
One size fits all.

Finished Measurements

Sweater
Bust 40 (45, 50, 55)"/101.5 (114, 127, 139.5)cm

Length 24 (25, 25½, 26)"/61 (63.5, 64, 65, 66)cm

Hat
Head circumference 22"/56cm (when slightly stretched)

Yarn
MONTERA by Classic Elite, 3½oz/100g hanks, each approx 127yd/116m (50% llama/50% wool) or a medium weight yarn

Sweater
• 9 (10, 11, 12) hanks in #3882 Bold Rose

Hat
• 2 hanks in #3882 Bold Rose

Needles & Notions
• One pair each sizes 7, 8, and 9 (4.5mm, 5mm, and 5.5mm) needles *or size needed to obtain gauge*

• Sizes 7 and 9 (4.5mm and 5.5mm) circular needles, 16"/40cm long

• Stitch markers

• Tapestry needle

• Stiff cardboard for winding tassel

Gauge
22 sts and 23 rows = 4"/10cm over openwork and rib pats using size 9 (5.5mm) needles.

Adjust the needle sizes as necessary to obtain correct gauge.

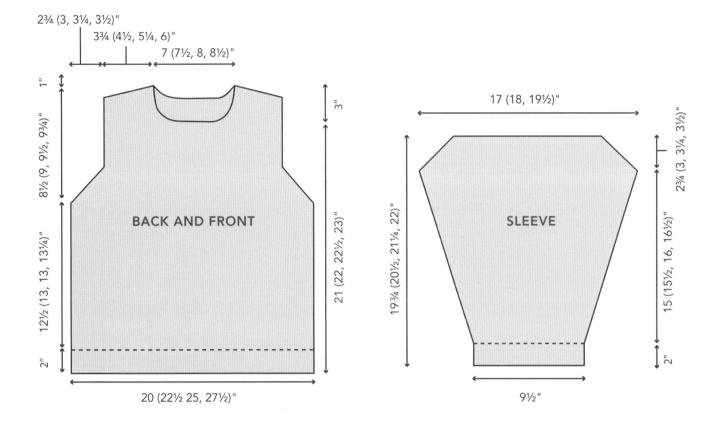

2¾ (3, 3¼, 3½)"

3¾ (4½, 5¼, 6)"

7 (7½, 8, 8½)"

1"

8½ (9, 9½, 9¾)"

12½ (13, 13, 13¼)"

2"

BACK AND FRONT

3"

21 (22, 22½, 23)"

20 (22½ 25, 27½)"

17 (18, 19½)"

2¾ (3, 3¼, 3½)"

19¾ (20½, 21¼, 22)"

15 (15½, 16, 16½)"

2"

SLEEVE

9½"

Notes
1) Slip markers every row.
2) Work all incs and decs one stitch in from edge.

▒ Reverse Stockinette Stitch
Row 1 (RS) Purl.
Row 2 Knit.
Rep Rows 1 and 2 for rev St st.

INSTRUCTIONS FOR THE SWEATER

Back
With size 8 (5mm) needles, CO 105 (117, 129, 141) sts.
Foundation row (WS) Work 3 (0, 0, 0) sts in rev St st, work Chart A over 0 (9, 15, 21) sts, pm, work rib section of Chart B over 99 sts, pm, work Chart A over 0 (9, 15, 21) sts, work 3 (0, 0, 0) sts in rev St st. Cont in pats as established until 12 rows are completed, end with a RS row. Change to size 9 (5.5mm) needles.
Setup rows (WS) Working sts before and after markers in pats as established, work 2 setup rows of Chart B over center 99 sts. Work even in pats

as established until piece measures 14½ (15, 15, 15¼)"/37 (38, 38, 39)cm from the beg, end with a WS row.

Armhole shaping
Dec 1 st each side *every* row 16 (16, 18, 18) times, then *every other* row 0 (1, 0, 1) time—73 (83, 93, 103) sts. Work even until armhole measures 8½ (9, 9½, 9¾)"/21.5 (23, 24, 25)cm, end with a WS row.

Neck and shoulder shaping
Next row (RS) Work across first 27 (31, 37, 41) sts, join a 2nd ball of yarn and BO center 19 (21, 19, 21) sts for back neck, work rem 27 (31, 37, 41) sts. BO 4 (4, 5, 5) sts at each neck edge twice. AT THE SAME TIME, BO at each shoulder edge 7 (7, 9, 11) sts once, then 6 (8, 9, 10) sts twice.

Front
Work as for back until piece measures 21 (22, 22½, 23)"/53.5 (56, 57, 58.5)cm from beg, end with a WS row.

CHART A

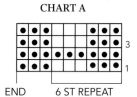

END   6 ST REPEAT

CHART B

REPEAT 20 ROWS
FOR BODY AND SLEEVE

TWO SET-UP ROWS

BODY AND SLEEVE RIB

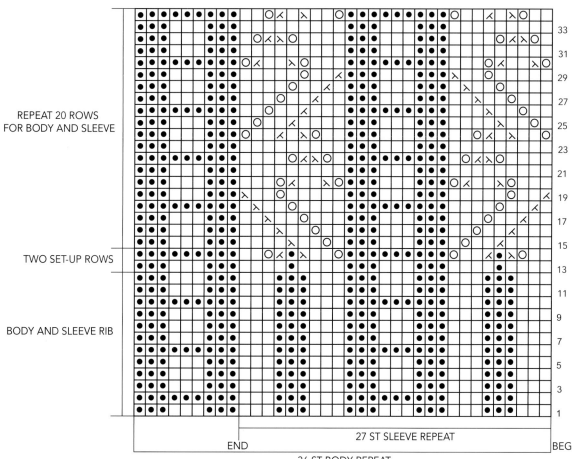

END

27 ST SLEEVE REPEAT

BEG

36 ST BODY REPEAT

KEY

☐ K ON RS, P ON WS

● P ON RS, K ON WS

SSK ON RS, SSP ON WS

K2TOG ON RS, P2TOG ON WS

O YARN OVER (YO)

Neck shaping

Next row (RS) Work across first 28 (33, 38, 43) sts, join a 2nd ball of yarn and BO center 17 sts, work rem 28 (33, 38, 43) sts. BO 3 sts at each neck edge 0 (1, 1, 2) times, 2 sts 3 (3, 3, 2) times, then 1 st 3 (1, 2, 2) time(s)—19 (23, 27, 31) sts each side. Work even until piece measures same length as back to shoulders. Shape shoulders as for back.

Sleeves

With size 7 (4.5mm) needles, CO 57 sts.
Setup row (WS) Work Chart A over 15 sts, pm, work rib section of Chart B over center 27 sts, pm, work Chart A over rem 15 sts. Cont in pats as established until 12 rows are completed, end with a RS row. Change to size 9 (5.5mm) needles.
Setup sleeve pats Cont to work Chart A before and after markers and work Chart B over center

27 sts, beg with the two setup rows. Maintaining pats as established, inc 1 st each side every 4th row 7 (12, 19, 21) times, then every 6th row 9 (6, 2, 1) times, working all new sts in Chart A pat as established—89 (93, 99, 101) sts. Work even until piece measures 17 (17 ½, 18, 18 ½)"/43 (44.5, 45.5, 47)cm. Mark beg and end of last row for beg of cap.

Cap shaping

Dec 1 st each side *every* row 14 (16, 18, 14) times, then *every other* row 0 (0, 0, 3) times. BO all sts loosely in pat.

FINISHING

Block pieces to measurements. Sew shoulder seams.

Turtleneck

With RS facing and smaller circular needle, pick up and k20 sts along left front neck, 17 sts of center front neck, 20 sts along right front neck and 39 (39, 45, 45) sts along back neck—96 (96, 102, 102) sts. Join, pm for beg of rnd. Work around in p3, k3 rib for 19 rnds; turtleneck should measure approx 3"/7.5cm from beg. Change to larger circular needle. Knit next rnd for turning ridge. Cont in rib pat as folls:
Rnds 1, 2, and 3 *K3, p3; rep from * around.
Rnd 4 Knit. Rep [Rnds 1–4] 5 times. BO all sts very loosely in rib. Set in sleeves. Sew side and sleeve seams.

INSTRUCTIONS FOR THE HAT

With size 9 (5.5mm) needles, CO 111 sts.
Row 1 (WS) K3, *p3, k3; rep from * to end.
Row 2 P3, *k3, p3; rep from * to end. Rep these 2 rows 5 times more, then Row 1 once. Purl next row for turning ridge. Change to size 7 (4.5mm) needles. Beg with Row 2, cont in rib pat for 13 more rows, end with a RS row. Change to size 9 (5.5mm) needles. Work Chart A for 25 rows; piece should measure approx 6"/15cm from turning ridge, end with Row 1.

Crown shaping

Row 26 P6, *p2tog, p10; rep from * to last 9 sts, end p2tog, p7—102 sts.
Row 27 K3, p3, *k2, p3, k3, p3; rep from * to last 8 sts, end k2, p3, k3.

Rows 28 and 29 Knit the k sts and purl the p sts as they appear.

Row 30 *P2 tog, p9; rep from * to last 3 sts, end p2tog, p1—92 sts.

Row 31 K2, *p3, k2; rep from * to end.

Rows 32 and 33 Rep Row 28.

Row 34 P2, *p2tog, p8; rep from * to last st, end p1—83 sts.

Row 35 *K2, p3, k2, p2; rep from * to last 2 sts, end k2.

Rows 36 and 37 Rep Row 28.

Row 38 P6, *p2tog, p7; rep from * to last 5 sts, p2tog, p3—74 sts.

Row 39 *K2, p2; rep from * to end.

Rows 40 and 41 Rep Row 28.

Row 42 P4, *p2tog, p6; rep from * to last 6 sts, end p2tog, p4—65 sts.

Row 43 K2, *p2, k1, p2, k2; rep from * to end.

Rows 44 and 45 Rep Row 28.

Row 46 *P2tog, p5; rep from * to last 2 sts, end p2tog—55 sts.

Row 47 *K1, p2; rep from * to last st, end k1.

Rows 48 and 49 Rep Row 28.

Row 50 P1, *p2tog, p4; rep from * to end—46 sts.

Row 51 *K1, p2, k1, p1; rep from * to last st, end k1.

Rows 52 and 53 Rep Row 28.

Row 54 *P3, p2tog; rep from * to last st, end p1—37 sts.

Row 55 *K1, p1; rep from * to last st, end k1.

Rows 56 and 57 Rep Row 28.

Row 58 [P2tog] 18 times, end p1—19 sts.

Rows 59–61 Rep Row 28.

Row 62 [P2tog] 9 times, p1—10 sts.

Row 63 [P2tog] 5 times—5 sts. Cut yarn, leaving a long tail. Thread tail in tapestry needle and weave through sts. Pull tight to gather, fasten securely, then sew seam, reversing seam over cuff.

Tassel

Wind yarn around a 5"/12.5cm piece of cardboard 100 times. Tie a double strand of yarn around one end and knot securely. Cut strands on opposite end. Wind yarn about 1"/2.5cm from tied end several times and weave in. Trim ends. Sew tassel to top of hat.

Designer Tip

Use a plastic CD case to wind tassels instead of the cardboard.

Alpacas

Alpacas have become the darlings of North American animal lovers. Alpacas, indigenous to the high Andes of Peru, Chile, and Bolivia, were first imported to the United States in 1984, where new owners have fallen in love with these gentle animals. Most feel they must have one or more in their lives, others raise them for the fiber, and still others raise them for breeding. At least $20,000+ a pop, the animals are not a small investment, but for many people, owning one or more alpacas is the best thing they have ever done in their lives. Many have made a switch from a fast-paced corporate life to raising alpacas.

Because these animals have adapted to living at a very high altitude in the Andes, where it can get very cold, they have evolved to produce a warm, soft, and luxurious fiber that is an absolute pleasure to wear. Like llamas, alpacas have medullated fibers, which means they are hollow. This traps air, creating very warm, insulating properties. Alpacas have a fine and lightweight fleece that does not retain water. In addition, their fleece prevents them from being overcome by the sun's heat. The fibers are about 15 to 18 microns in diameter.

There are two main types of alpacas, and they look very different. The Suri alpaca has a long, fine, and lustrous fiber that almost touches the ground. The Huacaya has a shorter, spongier, and crimpier fleece. Both breeds provide fiber that is luxurious and warm.

Alpacas stand about 3 feet tall at the shoulder and 4½ feet at their head. They weigh between 100 pounds (45kg)/(90kg) and 200 pounds (2–2.5kg). Every one or two years, the average alpaca produces about 4 to 6 pounds of fiber that can be used right away as it is almost free of guard hair. (The fiber of many of the other camelids must have the bristly guard hairs removed.)

When you knit with alpaca yarn, be aware that it will create a drapey fabric. To create a fabric that has a little more spring and shape to it, choose a yarn that is a blend of wool and alpaca.

CLASSIC ELITE

ORIGINALLY KNOWN AS ELITE AND HEADQUARTED IN THE HISTORIC textile center of Lowell, Massachusetts, in an old mill facility, Class Elite made a name for itself with its luxurious mohair yarns. Today, this widely distributed company (classiceliteyarns.com) offers more than 45 yarns, including wool and wool blends, cotton and cotton blends, alpaca, and angora—and they most recently added a merino/bamboo blend to their offerings. A luxury fiber division offers several different lines of yarn, including cashmere, baby camel, and silk. Owner Patricia Chew has developed a line of patterns. They also sell accessories and related products for the creative handknitter, crocheter, and weaver.

BLUE SKY ALPACAS

INSPIRED BY A PBS DOCUMENTARY ON ALPACAS AND THE LUXUROUS FIBERS THEY YIELD, FORMER graphic designer Linda Niemeyer quit her day job, bought a pregnant alpaca, and started a herd for herself. Although Linda now tends to a baby of her own, the alpacas have become pets, and the yarn business they inspired, Blue Sky Alpacas, is going strong. Linda shares her passion for high-quality fiber by designing exquisite, exclusive yarns for handknitters and offering them for sale at fine yarn shops across the United States. In addition to a range of alpaca-blended yarns (alpaca silk, alpaca merino), she also offers a line of beautiful organic cotton yarn. To find out what new heavenly yarns Linda is cooking up, visit blueskyalpacas.com.

The Alpaca Spectrum

According to the very active and enthusiastic Alpaca Owners and Breeders of America (www.alpacainfo.com), there are 22 registered colors of alpacas, from black to creamy white with roans, pintos, browns, red, fawns, rose grays, charcoal grays, and many other colors in between. The organization has been very strict about making sure that all the alpacas imported into the United States are registered. While more and more alpacas are being brought into the United States as well as being born in the country, 99 percent of the world's approximately three million alpacas are found in Peru, Bolivia, and Chile.

Arthur's Field of Dreams Sweater

DESIGNED BY CHARLOTTE QUIGGLE

What comes first: The fiber or the idea? For Charlotte, "usually the yarn talks and I listen."

As she knitted the swatch for "Arthur's Field of Dreams Sweater," she reflected upon her father, who had recently died. A doctor by trade, he had a lifelong fantasy of becoming a farmer, having worked on his grandfather's farm during the Depression. Upon retirement, he became a master gardener, bought a John Deere tractor, and moved to the country to get closer to the earth. Charlotte found the yarn "wanting" to become the furrows her father plowed and the baskets into which he would place his harvest.

Alpaca was her first choice; Charlotte has slept for years under an alpaca throw that was a gift from her father. She recognized that adding wool to the warm, soft alpaca would provide a lofty, elastic yarn. As it happened, both Blue Sky Alpacas and Charlotte make Minnesota their home, and Blue Sky has a sumptous alpaca-wool blend.

The sweater honors Charlotte's father in all ways: white because he was a doctor, the stitches because of the "farmer's" dreams, and the alpaca because he loved it.

Skill Level
Easy

Sizes
Instructions are for Men's Small. Changes for Medium, Large, and X-Large are in parentheses. (Shown in size Medium.)

Finished Measurements
Chest: 44 (48, 52, 56)"/112 (122, 132, 142)cm

Length: 25 (26, 26.5, 27)"/63.5 (66, 67, 68.5)cm

Yarn
BLUE SKY WORSTED by Blue Sky Alpacas 3.5oz/100g skeins, each approx 100yd/90m (50% alpaca/50% merino wool) or a medium weight yarn

• 11 (12, 13, 14) skeins #2003 Ecru

Needles & Notions
• One pair each sizes 9 and 10½ (5.5 and 6.5 mm) needles or *size needed to obtain gauge*

• Stitch holders

• Safety Pin

• Tapestry needle

Gauge
16 sts and 24 rows = 4"/10cm over Basketweave pat using larger needles.

Adjust the needle sizes as necessary to obtain correct gauge.

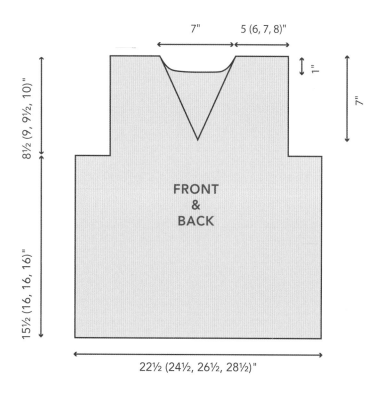

7"   5 (6, 7, 8)"

8½ (9, 9½, 10)"

1"

7"

FRONT
&
BACK

15½ (16, 16, 16)"

22½ (24½, 26½, 28½)"

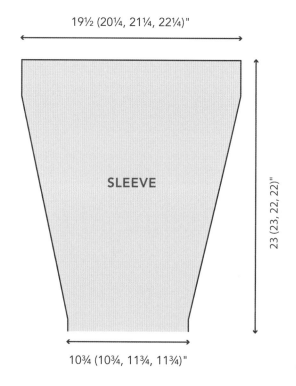

19½ (20¼, 21¼, 22¼)"

SLEEVE

23 (23, 22, 22)"

10¾ (10¾, 11¾, 11¾)"

Construction Notes

1) This garment is worked in flat pieces from the bottom up.

2) Work all incs 2 sts from edge.

3) Work decs as follows:

At beg of RS row, dec = ssk; at end of RS row, dec = k2tog.

At beg of WS row, dec = p2tog; at end of WS row, dec = ssp

GLOSSARY

⬛ **ssp** Slip next 2 sts k-wise one at a time, pass back to LH needle and p2tog tbl.

⬛ **2 st I-cord bindoff** With RS facing, CO on 2 sts at right end of needle using backwards loop method. *K1, ssk, DO NOT TURN. Slip 2 sts back to RH needle; rep from * until all sts are bound off—2 sts rem. Ssk, then fasten off.

⬛ **3-needle bindoff** Holding needles parallel with RS together and WS facing, k2tog from front and back needles, *k2tog from front and back needles and pass the first st over the second to bind off; rep from * across.

⬛ **Basketweave** (multiple of 8 sts + 2 selvedge sts)
Row 1 (RS) K1 [selv st],*k3, p5; rep from to last st, k1 [selv st].

Row 2 P1, *k5, p3; rep from * to last st, p1.
Row 3 Rep Row 1.
Row 4 Purl.
Row 5 K1, *p4, k3, p1; rep from *, to last st, k1.
Row 6 P1, *k1, p3, k4; rep from *, to last st, p1.
Row 7 Rep Row 5.
Row 8 Purl.
Rep Rows 1–8 for Basketweave pat.

3X1 GARTER RIB (multiple of 4 + 2 selvedge sts)
Row 1 (RS) K1 [selv st], *k3, p1; rep from * to last st, k1 [selv st].
Row 2 Purl.
Rep Rows 1 and 2 for 3x1 Garter Rib.

INSTRUCTIONS FOR THE SWEATER

Back

With smaller needles, CO 90 (98, 106, 114) sts. Work in St st for 6 rows.
Next Row (RS) Change to larger needles and Basketweave pat, working first and last sts in St st for selvedge. Work even until piece measures approx 9½"/24cm from beg, end with Row 4 or 8.
Next Row Beg Garter Rib, maintaining 1 selvedge st each side. Work even until piece measures

15½ (16, 16, 16)"/39.5 (40.5, 40.5, 40.5)cm or desired length to armhole, end with a WS row.

ARMHOLE SHAPING

BO 12 sts at beg of next row and 13 sts at beg of foll row—65 (73, 81, 89) sts. Work even until armhole measures 8½ (9, 9½, 10)"/21.5 (23, 24, 25)cm, end with a RS row.

BACK NECK SHAPING

Next row (WS) P25 (29, 33, 37), CO 1 st using backwards loop method, slip center 15 (15, 15, 15) sts to holder, join 2nd ball of yarn, CO 1 st using backwards loop method, purl to end—26 (30, 34, 38) sts each shoulder.
RS Dec Row Work to 9 sts before neck edge, k2tog, work to neck edge; with 2nd ball of yarn, work 7 sts, ssk, work to end.
WS Dec Row Work to 9 sts before neck edge, ssp, work to neck edge; with 2nd ball of yarn, work 7 sts, p2tog, work to end of row. Rep previous 2 rows 2 times more—20 (24, 28, 32) sts rem each shoulder. Place sts on seperate holders.

Front

Work as for back until armhole measures 2½ (3, 3½, 4)"/6.5 (7.5, 9, 10)cm, end with a RS row.

V-NECK SHAPING

Next row (WS) P32 (36, 40, 44), CO 1 st using backwards loop method, put next st on safety pin; join 2nd ball of yarn and CO 1 st using backwards loop method, work to end of row—33 (37, 41, 45) sts each side. Working both sides separately and at same time, work Dec row on next row, and then every 3rd row 12 times in same manner as for back neck—20 (24, 28, 32) sts each shoulder. Work even until armhole measures same length as back. Place sts on seperate holders.

Sleeves

Note *If making garment for a woman, adjust for shorter sleeve length by increasing at a more rapid rate.* With smaller needles, CO 43 (43, 47, 47) sts. Work in St st for 6 rows. Change to larger needles.
Setup row (RS) K, *p1, k3; rep from * to last 4 sts, end p, k3. Maintain first and last 2 sts in St st and cont in 3x1 Garter Rib as established. AT

SAME TIME, inc 1 st each side every 4th row 0 (1, 3, 7) times, every 6th row 12 (18, 16, 14) times, and every 8th row 5 (0, 0, 0) times, working new sts into pat—77 (81, 85, 89) sts. Work even until piece measures 23 (23, 22, 22)"/58.5 (58.5, 56, 56)cm or desired length. Loosely BO all sts.

FINISHING

Block to measurements.
Back Neck Slip back neck sts from holder to needle. With RS facing, work 2-st I-cord bind off.
Shoulder seams Slip shoulder sts from holders to needles and work 3-needle bind off.
Set in sleeves, sew underarm and side seams. With a tapestry needle, weave in loose yarn tails to the WS of work and secure.

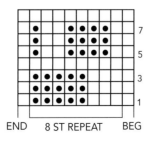

BASKETWEAVE STITCH

3 X 1 GARTER RIB

KEY

☐ K ON RS, P ON WS

▣ P ON RS, K ON WS

Vicunas

Many believe that vicunas are the wild ancestors of alpacas. These graceful animals live high in the Andes, above 13,000 feet (3,962m). Weighing about 100 pounds and standing less than 3 feet (.91m) at the shoulder, they are the smallest member of the camelid family. Vicunas have large round eyes; long slender necks; a white bib and little head or leg wool; and padded, cloven hooves. Their coat is dense and very fine, with a distinctive cinnamon–golden beige color.

Vicunas were nearly hunted to extinction by the late 1970s because their fleeces are so valuable. (At the age of three years old, one animal will produce only a pound of fleece.) At that time there were only 8,000 left in the Andes. Happily, due to conservation efforts, there are at least 125,000 vicunas in the Andes today. For many years vicuna fiber was not allowed to be sold because the animals were on the endangered species list. They are no longer considered to be endangered, and today they are trapped and sheared, as opposed to killed, as poachers had done. The high Andes is an economically challenged area, and now that the

locals are once again able to obtain vicuna fleece, this has become an income-generating industry for the people who live here.

The ancient community effort of trapping vicuna is called a chacu. What a sight it is to see villagers line up with a mile-long rope and chant and wave their arms as vicunas run parallel to the rope and into a trap. There the animals are shorn and then released. Once a vicuna has had a haircut, poachers are not as interested in it. Because the selling of vicuna fiber is no longer illegal, it is critical that we know where the fiber came from—a sanctioned chacu, rather than a poacher.

The very fine and soft fleece of the vicuna was valued by the ancient Incas, who held annual chacus to shear the animals. Only Inca royalty were allowed to wear garments spun from it. Commoners caught with vicuna fleece were executed. Although the last Inca ruler was killed by Spanish conquistadors in 1532, the reputation of vicuna fleece as a luxury fiber continues.

The animals themselves are endearing. They communicate by signaling one another with their ears, tails, and body positions. They also have a high-pitched whinny that can alert the herd. They "speak" to their friends with a soft humming sound and produce a range of other guttural sounds that signal anger and fear. Orgling is the male-only melodic mating sound that attracts the female vicuna.

PACO-VICUNAS
There is a new North American camelid that is being bred, the paco-vicuna. This animal blends

Vicuna fiber is about 11 microns, finer than the finest cashmere, which measures about 13 microns. Vicuna has exceptional insulating properties.

Like most other camelids, guanacos have a double-layered coat, with the outer layer being coarse.

the characteristics of alpaca with the high-quality of the vicuna, creating a fiber that is finer than alpaca—and even more expensive. Currently, only roving is available to handspinners.

Father Don Julio Cabrera was breeding paco-vicunas in Peru in the 1840s and they were released into the wild. In the mid-1960s, there was another brief test cross-breeding vicunas with alpacas in Peru. In 1998, Phil, Chris, and Dave Switzer of Switzer-Land Alpacas in Estes Park, Colorado, began importing specially selected alpacas from South America, their criterion being to obtain alpacas that had many of the characteristics of vicunas. The DNA of their hand-chosen alpacas was then tested to determine whether the animals were of vicuna heritage. Through careful breeding, the Switzers have created the North American breed of paco-vicunas. Their goal was to get animals that have the prized ultrafine and ultrasoft fiber of the vicuna—including the vicuna's unique color and volume of fiber—and a calmer alpaca temperament than that of the feisty vicunas, which do not adapt well to domestication. Paco-vicunas, in North America are registered through the Paco-Vicuna Registry (www.vicunaregistry.com).

Guanacos

Another rare South American camelid is the guanaco. Guanacos were once overhunted for their thick, warm fleece. Now they thrive in areas that are protected by law, mainly in the extreme south of the continent. About 500,000 live wild in the mountains of Argentina and Chile and the breed is almost extinct, with no more than 5,000 animals remaining in Peru. Guanacos live in groups with one male and five to ten females with their babies. They are very swift animals and good swimmers, able to swim between the islands of Patagonia and Tierra del Fuego.

These animals weigh somewhere in the range of 250 pounds (113.5kg) with a fiber measurement of about 18 microns. The animal is mainly light brown with black splotches on the head and white around the lips, ears, belly, and inner parts of the legs, which gives it a very contoured look.

Goats

Goats and sheep were among the earliest domesticated animals. Remains of the Bezoar goat of Asia Minor have been found that date back to 7,000 and 6,000 BC. Unlike sheep, goats will return to a wild state if given the chance.

ANGORA GOATS:
THE SOURCE OF MOHAIR

While they resemble sheep, angora goats are goats, and they are the source of strong, lustrous mohair. Unlike most sheep, which are rather fuzzy-looking, angora goats tend to have curly

Below
Angora goats are the source of shiny mohair.

locks instead of tightly crimped fibers. The fibers themselves are more compact and dense than wool, and mohair feels smoother and more slippery than wool to the touch. If you knit with a yarn that is 100 percent mohair, the garment can be heavy and stretch out (perhaps never to return to its original shape). However, yarn that is a mixture of mohair and wool has luster, lightness, and elasticity. Mohair has an appealing halo quality, and it will fluff out into open spaces. Think about knitting mohair and mohair/wool yarn on big needles so the yarn will bloom into the spaces between the stitches. This yarn also accepts dyes readily.

The angora goat was named for the ancient Turkish city of Angora, today known as Ankara, where the animal was first domesticated. The word *mohair* is thought to have been derived from the Arabic *mukhayyar*, which means choice or select.

Kept as pets, angora goats were not exported for centuries. However, in 1849, Dr. James B. Davis, an American who spent four years in Turkey helping local residents boost their cotton production, was given seven does and two bucks as gifts for his help. These seven goats marked the beginning of the mohair business in the United States. Today, over 90 percent of the mohair in the United States is produced in Texas, which also accounts for 40 percent of the world's supply of mohair. South Africa is the leading producer. The Mohair Council of America (www.mohairusa.com) is based in San Angelo, Texas, near the Edwards Plateau. The rugged, semi-arid ranching region is prime goat country, and the council claims that 90 percent of all U.S. angora goats live within a 150-mile (251km) radius of the national headquarters.

Goats are relatively small—75 to 125 pounds (34–57kg) when they are full grown—and both males and females have horns, with the horns being more pronounced on the males. They produce fiber at about one inch (1cm) per month and they tend to be shorn twice a year. Each shearing weighs from 3 to 5 pounds (1.4–2.3kg).

The age of the goat affects the diameter of the fiber. Kid mohair comes from the first clip when the goat is about six months old and the fiber is 23 to 30 microns. This is very soft, but does not have as much body and luster as the fiber from an older

goat, which is 25 to 45 microns. Kid mohair lends itself well to whatever soft garment you desire, be it baby booties or a hat-and-scarf set that will keep you warm—and comfortable.

Many people tend to think of mohair as a fiber to knit. However, it has many qualities that make it important for woven fabrics. It is durable, lustrous, naturally fire resistant, wrinkle resistant, and sound absorbent. These characteristics make it the perfect fiber to blend with wool to make carpets, drapes, and upholstery.

Opposite
The super, soft mohair locks (upper left) can be spun into yarns that vary in texture as illustrated by the skein and ball of mohair.

Below
Unspun mohair, available in a riot of colors, highlights the fiber's ability to absorb dye.

Goats of Many Colors

Some breeders specialize in colored angora goats. Goats classified as black can range from a deep solid black to a light gray or silver. These goats can have color patterning on their bodies as well. Goats designated as red range in color from copper to apricot. If you would like more information, visit the Colored Angora Goat Breeders Association online at (www.cagba.org).

Flirty Ruffle-Edged Scarf

DESIGNED BY BARBARA ALBRIGHT

A simple ribbed scarf takes on a whole new look when you add a whirly-swirly ruffle to each end. The first ruffle is created by casting on a large number of stitches and decreasing down to the width of the scarf. At the other end, a series of increases create the finishing ruffle. This curly scarf in mohair was a natural, given the author's fascination with the curly locks of the Angora goat—the source of mohair.

Skill Level	Finished Measurements	Yarn	Needles & Notions	Gauge
Easy	4½" x 62"/11.5 x 157.5cm	BOTANICAL SHADES, 2oz/56.75g skeins, each approx 118yd/108m (60% kid mohair/40% wool) or a medium weight yarn • 4 skeins in Poppy	• One pair size 8 (5mm) needles *or size needed to obtain gauge* • Tapestry needle	28 sts and 25 rows = 4"/10cm over k1, p1 rib using size 8 (5mm) needles. *Adjust the needle sizes as necessary to obtain correct gauge.*

BOTANICAL SHADES (formerly Tregellys Fiber Farm)

IN 1994, ED AND JODY COTHEY MOVED INTO THE DODGE FARMHOUSE IN HAWLEY, MASSACHUSETTS.

They named their new home Tregellys, which in Cornish means "hidden homestead." Their homestead turned into a farm when they traded their woodchipper for a couple of dairy goats and liked them so much they added two pigs and two Merino sheep.

It didn't stop there; over the years the Cotheys have added angora goats; llamas; alpacas; yaks; Icelandic, Navajo-Churro, Soay, Jacob, Shetland, and Karakul sheep; White Galloway cattle; Dzo and Dzomo; and Black Angus and Jersey cattle. And then there are the seven dogs, five cats, and varied ducks, geese, chickens, turkeys, pheasants, and peacocks. (Many of the photographs in *The Natural Knitter* were taken on-site at Tregellys.)

A former commercial fisherman, Ed Cothey now finds himself an avid weaver and self-proclaimed "fiber-holic."

Not only does Tregellys sell fine handwovens, they also use their animals as a springboard for educational programming. Tregellys fibers are now used in yarn marketed by Jody Cothey under the name Botanical Shades. The all–hand-dyed yarn uses natural botanical dyes, producing results that most large commercial manufacturers cannot achieve.

Designer Notes

1) You can make the scarf much shorter to create a fluffy, ruffled cravat-style scarf.
2) Add some zing and knit half the scarf using a contrasting or complementary color. Or knit the first and last two rows in a contrasting color.

GLOSSARY

▓ **k1f&b** Knit one in front and back of st.

INSTRUCTIONS

Scarf

CO 250 sts.

Beginning Ruffle
Row 1 and 3 (RS) Knit.
Rows 2 and 4 Purl.
Row 5 K2tog across—125 sts.
Rows 6 and 8 Purl.
Row 7 Knit.
Row 9 K2tog across, end k1—63 sts.
Rows 10 and 12 Purl.
Row 11 Knit.
Row 13 K2tog across, end k1—32 sts.

Rows 14 and 16 Purl.
Row 15 Knit. Cont in k1, p1 rib until piece measures 59½"/151cm from beg, or 2½"/6.5cm shorter than desired length, end with a WS row.

Ending ruffle

Rows 1 and 3 (RS) Knit.
Rows 2 and 4 Purl.
Row 5 K1f&b in each st across, end k1—63 sts.
Rows 6 and 8 Purl.
Row 7 Knit.
Row 9 K1f&b in each st across, end k1—125 sts.
Rows 10 and 12 Purl.
Row 11 Knit.
Row 13 K1f&b in each st across—250 sts.
Row 14 Purl.
Row 15 Knit.
Row 16 Purl. BO all sts.

FINISHING

With tapestry needle, weave in loose yarn tails to the WS of work and secure. Block as necessary.

Left
Cashmere provides "oohs" and "aahs" once you touch it and wear it. The Arc of the Covenant of the Old Testament supposedly was lined and curtained with cashmere. The unspun fiber shown comes from the soft undercoat on the sides and backs of cashmere-producing goats.

The Fiber of Kings
Cashmere, which grows softer with wear, historically was referred to as the "fiber of kings" for its warmth, softness, long wear, and high price tag. At 14 to 19 microns, it is considered to be eight times warmer than sheep's wool. Indigenous to the Himalayas, where mountain dwellers savor its extraordinary warmth, cashmere derives its name from the Kashmiri goats of the region. Cashmere goats living in these harsh mountainous climates produce the highest-quality fiber.

Cashmere

Many are surprised to learn that luscious cashmere comes from a goat, and not just one breed of goat. It can come from any of the down-bearing breeds. Cashmere refers to the actual fiber itself, and whether the fiber can be called *cashmere* lies in the skilled hands of the person who feels the fiber and classes it—deeming the downy, soft undercoat lovely enough to earn the name *cashmere.*

Most of the world's supply of cashmere is produced in Afghanistan, Iran, Outer Mongolia, India, and China. Because of the political disarray in these countries, in recent years other options have been explored and for more than fifteen years, Australia and New Zealand have been producing cashmere. It is a fairly new industry in the United States; the first cashmere goats were imported from Australia and New Zealand in the late 1980s.

As with many other animals, these goats have coarser guard hairs and downy, soft undercoats that are used to spin luxurious fibers (14 to 19 microns). Cashmere is the soft undercoat on the sides and backs of cashmere-producing goats. The luxurious down fibers are either removed by shearing or combing once a year in the spring when the animals molt. The colors can range from pure white to white with color and browns as well as grays and red.

The downy undercoat grows from midsummer through winter and varies in quality depending on the climate and nutrients on which the goat was raised. Longer guard hairs protect the soft downy cashmere undercoat, which is shorn each spring. Each goat produces only 3 to 8 ounces (85–227g) of cashmere down a year. This means that it would take three or more goats to produce enough fiber for a simple single-ply sweater.

Architectural Rib Pullover

DESIGNED BY NORAH GAUGHAN

A master of unique construction, Norah Gaughan designed this sweater as a continuation of her ongoing work in out-of-the-ordinary sweater construction. She says, "Creating a sweater with a cable crossing of large ribs as the focal point was my first thought. Then I had to figure out what would lead up to the center and what would spring forth from it."

Norah pays attention to what is happening on the runways, and she wanted to keep the design simple but with an interesting hem. She selected a lovely yarn from Harrisville Designs, which is 50 percent cashmere and 50 percent wool. Wool adds definition to the structural patterning, and cashmere is warm, soft, and lightweight. The cabled design on the front is repeated on the back.

Skill Level
Experienced

Sizes
Instructions are for Small. Changes for Medium and Large are in parentheses. Shown in size Medium.

Finished Measurements
Bust 38 (42, 46)"/96.5 (106.5, 116.75)cm

Length 22½ (23, 23½)"/57 (58.5, 59.5)cm

Yarn
CASHMERE BLEND by Harrisville Designs, 1¾oz/50g skeins, each approx 190yd/174m (50% cashmere/50% fine wool) or a light weight yarn

• 6 (7, 8) skeins in #8056 Taupe

Needles & Notions
• One pair each sizes 3 and 4 (3.25 and 3.5mm) needles *or size needed to obtain gauge*

• Size 3 (3.25mm) circular needle, 16"/40cm long

• One size 4 (3.5mm) double-pointed needle (dpn) for turning large cable

• Stitch markers

• Stitch holders

• Safety pins

• Tapestry needle

Gauge
23 sts and 34 rows = 4"/10cm over St st using larger needles.

Adjust the needle size as necessary to obtain correct gauge.

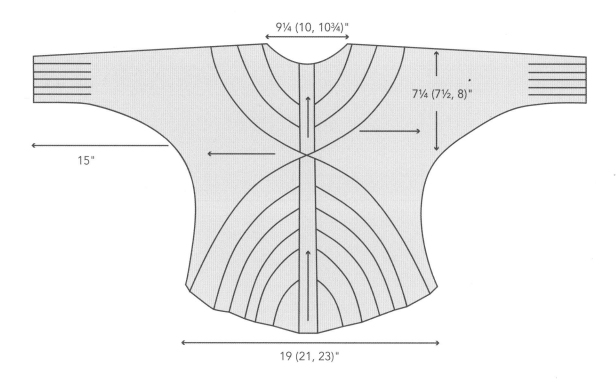

9¼ (10, 10¾)"

7¼ (7½, 8)"

15"

19 (21, 23)"

Construction Notes

1) This garment is made starting at the center front bottom.

2) The ribbed fabric is decreased at either side of a central rib, a large "cable" is turned at the center, after which the fabric is increased back out at either side of the central rib (this looks like an hourglass).

3) The piece is split for the front neck, worked over the shoulder, and then rejoined for the back, which is worked down from the shoulders in the reverse order of the front.

4) The sides are picked up from the edges of the "hourglass" and worked in St st (with shaping) out to the seams and sleeves, which are worked down to the long ribbed cuff.

5) The turtleneck is worked last.

GLOSSARY

⊠ **Cable row (RS)** P3, place 18 sts on dpn and hold in *back*, k12, slip last 6 sts from dpn back to LH needle and knit them, k12 sts from dpn, p3. (**Note:** *This is very tight.*)

⊠ **P-inc row (RS)** Work in rib as established to 1 st before marker, M1 p-wise, slip marker, k6, M1 p-wise, rib to end.

⊠ **K-1inc row (RS)** Work in rib as established to 1 st before marker, M1, slip marker, k6, M1, rib to end.

INSTRUCTIONS FOR SWEATER

Center Front Section

With larger needles, CO on 144 sts.

Setup pats (RS) P3, k12, [p4, k6] 5 times, p4, k1, pm, k5, [p4, k6] 5 times, p4, k12, p3.

Next and all WS rows Knit the k sts and purl the p sts as they appear. Work next 2 rows even.

Dec row (RS) Work in rib pat as established to 2 sts before marker, k2tog, k4, ssk, rib to end. Rep Dec row every RS row 53 times more—36 sts. Work next 7 rows even. Work Cable row. Work next 7 rows even. Cont shaping as folls: *work

P-Inc row every RS row 4 times, then K-inc Row every RS row 6 times—56 sts*. Rep from * to * once more, then work K-inc row once more, then work 1 row even—78 sts.

Divide for neck

Next row (RS) Work across first 36 sts, place next 6 sts on a holder, join a 2nd ball of yarn, work to end. Working both sides at once, work even for 4½ (5, 5½)"/11.5 (12.5, 14)cm, end with a WS row. Mark beg and end of last row for shoulders.

Center Back Section

Neck shaping

Next row (RS) Work across first 35 sts, p1, CO 4 sts at neck edge; with 2nd ball of yarn, p1, work in rib as established across last 35 sts.

Next row Work to neck edge, CO 4 sts, with 2nd ball of yarn k5, work in rib as established to end.

Next row Work to neck edge, CO 4 sts, with 2nd ball of yarn p5, work in rib as established to end.

Next row Work to neck edge, CO 4 sts, with 2nd ball of yarn, k9, work in rib as established to end.

Joining

Next row (RS) Work to neck edge, CO 22 (26, 30) sts for back neck, with same ball of yarn, p9 (drop 2nd ball of yarn), work in rib as established to end—110 (114, 118) sts.

Next row Rib 34 sts, pm, p1, k17 (19, 21), p6, k17 (19, 21), rib 35 sts. Work next 2 rows even.

Dec row (RS) Rib 34 sts, ssk, work to 2 sts before marker, k2tog, work to end. Rep Dec row every RS row 16 (18, 20) times more—76 sts.

Next row Work 40 sts, pm (remove previous marker), work to end.

Center Dec row (RS) Work to 2 sts before marker, k2tog, k4, ssk, work to end. Rep Center Dec row every RS row 19 times more—36 sts. Work next 7 rows even. Work Cable row, then work 7 rows even. Cont shaping as folls: work P-inc rows and K-inc rows as for center front from * to * 5 times, then work P-inc row 4 times more—144 sts. Work next 3 rows even. Bind off all sts. (**Note:** *On all side edges, mark Cable row.*)

Side and Sleeve

With RS facing and larger needles, beg at bottom side edge of front. Pick up and k 76 (78, 80) sts evenly spaced to cable marker, pm, 55 (60, 65) sts to pin-marked shoulder, 55 (60, 65) sts to cable marker on back, pm, then 76 (78, 80) sts to bottom edge—262 (276, 290) sts. (**Note:** *Shoulder markers can now be removed.*) Purl next row. Cont in St st to cuff as folls:

For size Small only

Proceed to "For all sizes."

For sizes Medium and Large only

Work 2 rows even.

Next row (RS) [Knit to 2 sts before marker, ssk, sm, k2tog] twice, knit to end. Purl next row even. Rep last 2 rows once more for Medium and 3 times more for Large—268 (274) sts.

For all sizes

*BO 2 sts at the beg of the next 2 rows.

Next 2 rows (BO and dec in center) BO 2 sts, [knit to 2 sts before marker, ssk, sm, k2tog] twice, knit to end of row. Turn, BO 2 sts, purl to end of row*; rep from * to * 13 times more—94 (100, 106) sts. Cont shaping as folls: BO 2 sts at the beg of the next 2 rows, then BO 4 sts at the beg of the foll 2 rows—82 (88, 94) sts.

Begin sleeve

Dec row (RS) K1, k2tog, knit to last 3 sts, ssk, k1. Rep Dec row every 4th row 17 (18, 17) times more—48 (52, 60) sts. Work even until sleeve measures 9"/23cm, end with a RS row. Change to smaller needles. Purl next row, dec 2 sts evenly spaced—46 (50, 58). Work in k2, p2 rib for 6"/15cm for cuff. BO all sts loosely in rib.

FINISHING

Steam or wet-block to measurements. Sew side and sleeve seams.

Neckband

Beg at center back neck. With RS facing and circular needle, pick up and k50 (54, 58) sts, k6 sts from holder, pick up and k52 (56, 60) sts to end—108 (116, 124) sts.

Rnd 1 [P2, k2] 12 (13, 14) times, p2, k6, [p2, k2] 13 (14, 15) times. Work even in rib pat for 4"/10cm. BO all sts loosely in rib. With a tapestry needle, weave in loose yarn tails to the WS of work and secure.

HARRISVILLE DESIGNS

THE BRICK MILL TOWN OF HARRISVILLE IS NESTLED INTO THE MONADNOCK HIGHLANDS OF SOUTHWESTERN New Hampshire and it is perhaps the only industrial American community of the early nineteenth century that still survives in its original form. In 1977, the Department of Interior designated Harrisville as a National Historic Landmark.

Harrisville Designs was established in 1971 with the goal of preserving the textile heritage and economic vitality that had sustained the village for almost two hundred years. They started by handweaving yarns and then branched out into making handweaving looms and equipment. In the late 1980s, they branched out further, creating Friendly Loom Products, a line of educational toys to introduce children to the joys of working with their hands.

Harrisville Designs is a small, family-owned and -operated business. The owners insist on quality, even for the smallest product. They love sharing their textile traditions with the world, and will continue their sustainable tradition for years to come.

Pygora Goats

Pygmy goats are small goats with a soft downy coat, and the angora goat produces mohair. In the 1970s, Katherine Jorgenson of Oregon crossbred an angora goat with a pygmy goat with the goal of getting fine fiber for handspinning. Since that time, the breed, called pygora goats, has expanded. Pygora goats have been embraced by small family farms and by 4-H kids, and there is even a Pygora Goat Breeders Association (see page 184).

This type of yarn is not widely available, but if you should ever feel it, you will know what it is!

Yaks

A fairly common fiber, yak has traditionally been woven into coverings for huts, blankets, mats, and sacks by Asians because of abundant herds in the region.

Members of the cattle family, these huge, shaggy beasts thrive in large domestic and small wild populations in Central Asia and India. Today, the wild yak, once abundant on the Tibetan plateau north of the Himalayas, is endangered because of uncontrolled hunting. The fiber used in yarns comes from the domestic yak (smaller than the wild yak), which number about 12 million in the high plateaus and mountains of Central Asia. However, more ranchers in the United States are adding yaks to their herds! Mostly these are people who are interested in alternative livestock.

One rancher, Phil Wykle of Kooskin, Idaho, was charmed by the animals and added them to his cattle ranch, realizing they do not require any different treatment from his cattle. Yaks are classified as cattle and so do not require any special permits. They also adjust readily to living at lower altitudes. Phil appreciated the versatility of yaks. They can be ridden like horses, packed like mules, and used to pull plows or carts. They are also a source of milk products and low-fat, low-cholesterol meat, which is beeflike but more delicate-tasting, perhaps similar to buffalo meat. Like buffalo, yaks can be cross-bred with cattle. Phil has selected yaks that are extra woolly and harvests their wool every year.

The yak has developed a thick coat of long hair that reaches almost to the ground and has a

micron count of 15 to 19. Most yaks are either black or very dark brown, but domestic yaks may also be golden-colored and have white markings from cross-breeding with cattle.

Arctic Musk Ox/Qiviut

It's difficult to believe that the rugged-looking Arctic musk ox can produce the the soft and luxurious fiber called qiviut. Known as *oomingmak* (the bearded one) to the Alaska Yupiit people, the musk ox lives in remote areas of Greenland, Alaska, and Canada, and is one of the few animals capable of living year-round in the Arctic climate. Its luscious underwool is very soft and fine (11 to 13 microns) and it is purported to be eight times warmer than sheep's wool. This layer of fluff

Opposite
Shown is the unspun natural colored fibers that come from the coat of the yak, and the yarn that it spins into.

Above left
The yak, a member of the bovine family, makes its home in Tibet and south central Asia. Standing about 6 feet (1.8 meters) at the shoulder, the shaggy beasts can be either brown or black.

Below left
The musk ox, also of the bovine family, is native to the Arctic tundra. They stand about 5 to 6 feet (1.5 to 1.8 meters) high at the shoulder and produce a coat that is a mixture of brown, gray, and yellow, with guard hairs that nearly touch the ground.

Qiviut Fiber

Musk ox shed their fleece once a year in the spring, grow a new layer by fall, and produce between five and seven pounds (2–3kg)of fleece a year in shades ranging from light brown to white and dark brown to almost black. Given the small harvest, the qiviut yarn is typically spun in co-ops or cashmere factories. Because the fleece is so fine and has long guard hairs that require removal, processing it into fibers can be very challenging.

Availability of the fiber is limited, so it's pricey: two ounces (57g) cost $80— enough to knit one hat. But it will be one of the softest, warmest, and most lightweight hats you will ever own. And it won't shrink in hot water!

Opposite
Who could imagine that the musk ox would produce such a wonderfully soft fiber that can be knit into such extremely warm and lightweight garments.

OOMINGMAK

APPROXIMATELY 250 NATIVE Alaskan women from remote coastal villages joined together to create handknit items using qiviut, which is available online at www.qiviut.com or at their Anchorage store. They mostly sell finished handknitted items, but they do have a handknitting hat kit. The business provides some much-needed income for these women.

protects the animal from temperatures of –100°F (–73°C). In fact, captive herds must be protected from overheating when the temperatures rise to 70°F (21°C). In the 1930s, the musk ox were hunted almost to extinction in Alaska and they were designated as threatened on the mainland of Canada. The musk ox continues to be an endangered species.

Today there are a few musk ox farms in existence—one at the University of Alaska and another at the University of Saskatchewan—and some fiber has been hand-gathered from the Arctic tundra. Unlike the other "beasts" that are hand shorn, the "powder puff" fleece from musk ox is shed and either hand-collected on the tundra or combed out in the case of domestication. Hand-combed qiviut from farmed musk ox is softer and cleaner than the undercoat shed in the wild, since the loose fiber is not subjected to the harsh climate.

However, most of the qiviut yarn that is available today comes from an annual government-controlled hunt in Canada. Anyone who receives a permit specifically for the musk ox can hunt the animals, including the Inuit people who have traditionally done so for centuries. This sustainable resource can be a substantial benefit to the residents of Arctic communities.

MINI-MILLS LTD.

IN ASSOCIATION WITH ITS SISTER
company, International Spinners
Ltd., Mini-Mills designs and manu-
factures fiber processing machines.
Located on Prince Edward Island,
Canada, it is becoming recognized
worldwide for the advanced
technology incorporated into its
specialized machinery.

There are many types of fiber—all
with different spinning needs—and
these convenient machines are
the perfect solution! They can spin
specialty fibers to requirements.
Also, since mills are not always
readily available near the fiber-
producing animals, these machines
are welcome ways of getting to the
finished yarn. The fiber can be spun
into yarn close to where it is grown
without having to transport it to a mill.

If you are interested in purchasing
a fiber processing machine for
yourself, the owners of Mini-Mills
recommend that you visit them first
to see what their machines can do.
Then they will set up the machines
at the desired location and you will
receive more training.

In addition to manufacturing mill
equipment, Mini-Mills Ltd. also sells
yarn and fibers, including the yarn
in Linda Romens's Qiviut Twinset.

Qiviut Twinset

DESIGNED BY LINDA ROMENS

As far as qiviut, Linda says, it was love at first touch. The first time she touched qiviut was at a Stitches Knitting conference. Because of its cost, she felt pure qiviut yarn was prohibitively expensive to use for anything larger than a scarf, so she was forced to love it from afar. In this project, she used a qiviut/wool/alpaca blend that is not as expensive as pure qiviut but is still extraordinarily soft. Linda also found that this blend was actually more economical to work with than she imagined because qiviut has a lot of loft, and weighs next to nothing. The cardigan weighs 8 ounces (227g) and the vest weighs a mere 3 ounces (85g). The next time you are shivering in front of the computer, put on this cardigan and you'll warm right up!

Skill Level
Experienced

Sizes
Instructions are for X-Small. Changes for Small, Medium, and Large are in parentheses. Shown in size X-Small.

Finished Measurements

Vest
Bust 32 (35½, 39, 42¾)"/81(90, 99, 108.5)cm

Length 17¼ (19½, 21½, 23½)"/ 44 (49.5, 54.5, 59.5)cm

Cardigan
Bust (buttoned) 35 (38½, 42¼, 45¾)"/89 (97.5, 107.5, 116)cm

Length 19¾ (22¼, 24½, 27)"/50 (56.5, 62, 68.5)cm

Yarn
NORTHERN MIST spun by Mini Mills Ltd., 2oz/57g skeins, each approx 275yd/253m (33% qiviut/33% merino/33% alpaca) or a light weight yarn

Vest
• 2 (3, 3, 4) skeins in Natural Light Gray

Cardigan
• 4 (5, 6, 8) skeins in Natural Light Gray

Needles & Notions
• Size 5 (3.75mm) circular needle, 24"/60cm long *or size needed to obtain gauge*

• Size F/5 (3.75mm) crochet hook

• Waste yarn for yarn markers

• Stitch holders

• Tapestry needle

• 5 (5, 6, 6) 1¼"/32mm buttons

Gauge
18 sts and 26 rows = 4"/10cm over lace pat using size 5 (3.75mm) needle (after blocking).

Adjust the needle size as necessary to obtain correct gauge.

Gauge Swatch
CO 22 sts. K2, work X-Small Chart (18-st rep plus 1), k2. Maintain 2 edge sts each side in garter st and work entire 32 rows of chart. Block to "open up" lace before measuring.

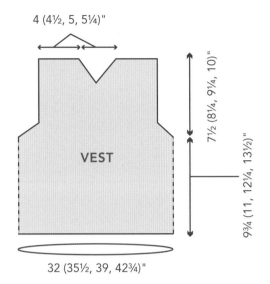

4 (4½, 5, 5¼)"

VEST

7½ (8¼, 9¼, 10)"

9¾ (11, 12¼, 13½)"

32 (35½, 39, 42¾)"

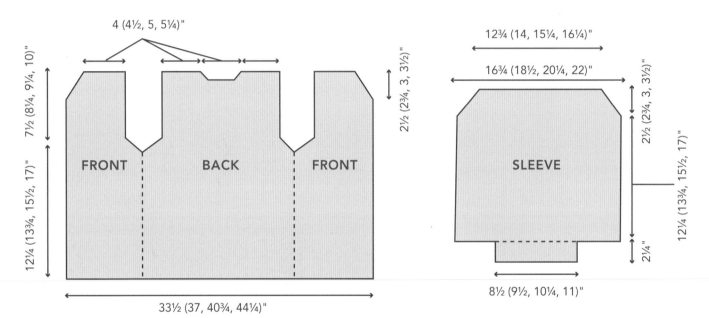

4 (4½, 5, 5¼)"

7½ (8¼, 9¼, 10)"

12¼ (13¾, 15½, 17)"

FRONT

BACK

FRONT

2½ (2¾, 3, 3½)"

33½ (37, 40¾, 44¼)"

12¾ (14, 15¼, 16¼)"

16¾ (18½, 20¼, 22)"

SLEEVE

2½ (2¾, 3, 3½)"

12¼ (13¾, 15½, 17)"

2¼"

8½ (9½, 10¼, 11)"

Construction Notes

VEST

1) The vest is worked in the round from the bottom up, then divided at the armholes.

2) The scalloped edges are formed by working short rows back and forth within the ribbed sections of the first pat rep, one "scallop" at a time.

3) Armhole and neck shaping are accomplished by working the first and last decreases of the lace st and eliminating the paired yarn over.

4) All edge sts are worked in St st.

5) The chart is worked 3 times.

CARDIGAN

1) The cardigan is worked back and forth in one piece from the bottom up, then divided at the armholes.

2) The scalloped edges are formed in the same manner as for the vest.

3) Armhole and neck shaping are accomplished in the same manner as for the vest.

4) The bands and collar are worked in a dense linen st with one-row bound buttonholes.

5) All edge sts are worked in St st.

6) The chart is worked 4 times.

GLOSSARY

3-needle bindoff Holding needles parallel with RS together and WS facing, k2tog from front and back needles, *k2tog from front and back needles and pass the first st over the second to bind off; rep from * to end.

Lace Pattern Stitch Lace pat st has 18 (20, 22, 24) st rep. See chart for size being worked.

Vest
Beg at st indicated on Row 1.

Cardigan
Beg at st indicated on Row 17 (19, 21, 23).

Linen Stitch (over an even number of sts)
Row 1 (WS) P1, *sl 1 wyib, p1; rep from *, end p1.
Row 2 K1, *sl 1 wyif, k1; rep from *, end k1.
Rep Rows 1 and 2 for Linen st.

"Scalloping" Short Rows (worked on rnds with green and red marked sts)
*Work through *green* st on chart. Wyif, slip the next st, bring yarn to back, then slip the st back to LH needle. Turn, and working the sts as they present themselves (k or p tbl), work back through *red* st on chart. Wyib, slip the next st, bring yarn forward and slip the st back to the LH needle. Work across to next pat rep; rep from *. Cont in this manner, working short rows in each ribbed section of pat rep, then work to end of rnd. On the next rnd, work the wraps tog with the wrapped st.

One-row bound buttonhole
(worked over 5 sts)
1) With yarn in front, slip next st. Yarn back, slip 2nd st. Drop the yarn.
2) Pass the first slipped st over the 2nd slipped st . Slip another st and pass the previous slipped st over it. Rep 3 more times.
3) Pass the last slipped st back to the LH needle. Turn work.
4) With yarn in back, cable CO 5 sts.
5) CO one more st, but bring the yarn to the front between this extra st and the last buttonhole st before placing the extra st on the LH needle. Turn work.
6) Slip a st from the LH needle, pass the extra st over the slipped st and tighten the extra st firmly.

INSTRUCTIONS FOR THE VEST

Lower body
Using long-tail method, CO 145 (161, 177, 193) sts. Taking care not to twist sts on needle, join rnd by slipping the first st of the rnd to the RH needle and passing the last st over—144 (160, 176, 192) sts. Place yarn marker for beg of rnd. Knit 1 rnd.
Next 2 rnds Work first 2 rnds lace pat.
Next rnd Work Rnd 3 of lace pat, working "scalloping" short rows in ribbed area as indicated. Cont working lace pat, working short rows on rnds indicated with red/green marked sts. After working 3 (3, 4, 4) sets of short rows, work lace pat without further short rows until all rnds of lace pat have been worked twice.

Armhole shaping
Next rnd BO 3 sts, work to end of 4th pat rep, *but do not work yo*, BO 4 sts, work to end of rnd (you will end with a k2tog). Put sts for back on holder and beg working back and forth on front.

Front
Next row (WS) Work across in pat as established, CO 1 st at each end of row for edge sts.
Next row K1 (edge st), ssk, cont in pat as established across, end k2tog, k1 (edge st).

CHART FOR X-SMALL

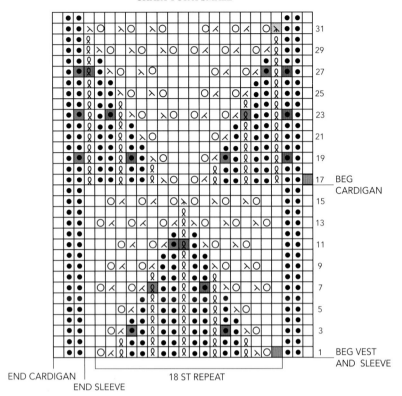

END CARDIGAN
END SLEEVE
18 ST REPEAT
BEG CARDIGAN
BEG VEST AND SLEEVE

(**Note:** *Work edge sts in St st throughout; by working ssk and k2tog at armhole edges without a compensating yo, the row will be dec by 1 st at each edge.*) Cont in this manner until Row 16 (18, 20, 22) is completed. Cont working pat, without dec at the armhole edge, until all rows of the pattern have been completed—57 (63, 69, 75) sts.

Neck shaping

Next row (RS) Work until 2nd k2tog has been worked, join a 2nd ball of yarn, BO next 2 sts, work to end.

Next row CO 1 st at each neck edge for edge sts and work these sts in St st throughout. Working both sides at the same time in pat as established, end and beg RS rows at the neck edges with k2tog, k1 (edge st), and ssk, k1 (edge st) until 21 (23, 25, 27) sts rem each side, end with a WS row.

Shoulder shaping

BO 11 (12, 13, 14) sts at beg of next 2 rows once, then 10 (11, 12, 13) sts once.

Back

Work as for front.

FINISHING

Block piece to measurements. Sew shoulder seams.

Neck edging

With RS facing and crochet hook, join yarn with a sl st in center back neck. **Rnd 1** Ch 1, making sure that work lies flat, sc evenly around entire edge, join rnd with a sl st in first sc. Do not turn. **Rnd 2** Ch 1, work rev sc (also known as Crab St) in opposite direction in each st around, join rnd with a sl st in first sc. Fasten off.

Armhole edging

With RS facing and crochet hook, join yarn with a sl st in underarm seam. Rep Rnds 1 and 2 as for neck edging.

INSTRUCTIONS FOR THE CARDIGAN

Body

CO 151 (167, 183, 199) sts. Purl 1 row.
Next row Beg on Row 17 (21, 23, 25), k1, p2, work 8 reps of lace pat foll appropriate chart for size, end p2, k1.

CHART FOR SMALL

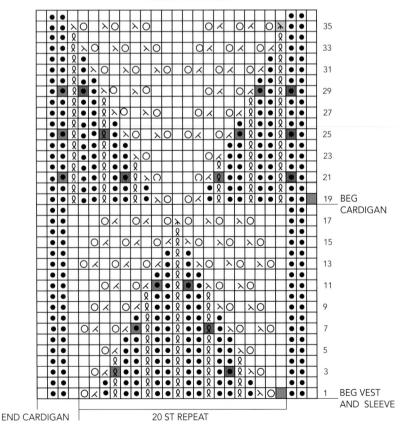

END CARDIGAN
END SLEEVE
20 ST REPEAT
BEG CARDIGAN
BEG VEST AND SLEEVE

Next row K1, p2, work lace pat as established across, end p2, k1.

Next (short) row Work Row 19 (23, 25, 27) of lace pat, working "scalloping" short rows in ribbed area as indicated. Cont working lace pat, working short rows on rows indicated with red/green marked sts. After working 3 (3, 4, 4) sets of short rows, work lace pat without further short rows until chart has been worked 2½ times, end on row 32 (36, 40, 44).

Divide for armholes

Work as established through the "k2tog" st of the 2nd pat rep and slip sts just worked to holder for front; *do not work yo*, BO 1 st, ssk, then work as established until the "k2tog" of the 6th patt rep, BO 1 st, *do not work yo*, ssk, work to end of row. Cut yarn and slip sts worked from bindoff to end of row to a holder for other front.

Back

Next row (WS) Join a new ball of yarn at beg of row for back, CO 1 st at each end of row for edge sts and work pat as established.

Next row K1 (edge st), ssk, cont in pat as established across row, end k2tog, k1 (edge st). (**Note:** Work edge sts in St st throughout, by working ssk and k2tog at armhole edges without a compensating yo, the row will be dec by 1 st at each edge.) Cont in this manner through Row 16 (18, 20, 22)—57 (63, 69, 75) sts. Work even through Row 10 (12, 14, 16) of the 4th rep.

Neck shaping

Next row Work 22 (24, 26, 28) sts, join a 2nd ball of yarn and BO next 13 (15, 17, 19) sts for back neck, work to end of row.

Next row CO 1 edge st at each neck edge and cont working pat as established, shaping the neck edges as before, until the rem rows of the 4th rep of the pat have been worked—21 (23, 25, 27) sts each side. Place sts on holders.

Right Front

Next row (WS) Slip sts from holder to needle and work pat as established, casting on 1 edge st at armhole edge. Work armhole shaping as for back, then work even through Row 32 (36, 40, 44)—32 (35, 38, 41) sts.

CHART FOR MEDIUM

39
37
35
33
31
29
27
25
23
21 BEG CARDIGAN
19
17
15
13
11
9
7
5
3
1 BEG VEST AND SLEEVE

END SLEEVE
22 ST REPEAT
END CARDIGAN

KEY

☐ K ON RS, P ON WS

● P ON RS, K ON WS

ℚ K TBL ON RS, P TBL ON WS

O YARN OVER (YO)

﹨ SSK ON RS, SSP ON WS

⁄ K2TOG ON RS, P2TOG ON WS

⋏ SL 1 ST, K2TOG, PSSO

⋌ ON CARDIGAN ONLY: K2TOG AT BEG OF ROW

▨ WITH RS FACING, WYIF, SLIP THE NEXT ST, BRING THE YARN TO BACK, THEN SLIP THE ST BACK TO LH NEEDLE. TURN.

▥ WITH WS FACING, WYIB, SLIP THE NEXT ST, BRING THE YARN FORWARD AND SLIP THE ST BACK TO LH NEEDLE. TURN AND WORK ACROSS TO NEXT PAT REP.

▨ BEGIN WITH THIS STITCH

CHART FOR LARGE

Chart row numbers (right side): 43, 41, 39, 37, 35, 33, 31, 29, 27, 25, 23 — BEG CARDIGAN, 21, 19, 17, 15, 13, 11, 9, 7, 5, 3, 1 — BEG VEST AND SLEEVE

Labels: END CARDIGAN, END SLEEVE, 24 ST REPEAT

Neck shaping

Next row (RS) BO 3 sts, *do not work yo,* ssk, then work to last k2tog, *do not work yo,* work to end of row (the first st is now edge st).

Next row BO 3 sts, then work to end of row. Work neck shaping as for armholes, ending on Row 16 (18, 20, 22)—21 (23, 25, 27) sts. Place sts on holder.

Left Front

Work as for right front, reversing all shaping.

Sleeves

CO 43 (47, 51, 55) sts. Work k1, p1 rib for 2¼"/5.5cm, end with a RS row.

Next row (WS) Purl across and inc 32 (36, 40, 44) sts evenly spaced—75 (83, 91, 99) sts. Maintaining first and last sts (edge sts) in St st, work appropriate chart 2½ times, ending on Row 15 (17, 19, 21).

Next row BO 3 sts, work to end.
Next row BO 2 sts, slip st back to LH needle, then beg row with the first ssk, cont to end of row. CO 1 st each end for edge sts and work pat as established to row 32 (36, 40, 44), beg the RS rows with ssk, and ending with k2tog, *without working the yarn overs* (2 sts dec every other row)— 57 (63, 69, 75) sts. Working in St st, BO 18 (20, 22, 24) sts at beg of next 2 rows. BO off rem sts.

FINISHING

Block pieces to measurements. Join shoulders using 3-needle bindoff. Set in sleeves. Sew under-arm seams.

Buttonband

(**Note:** Linen st used for the bands has a tighter gauge than lace pat st.) With RS facing, pick up an even number of sts (approx 19 sts per 20 rows) evenly spaced along left front edge. Work in Linen st for 15 rows. BO all sts firmly.

Buttonhole band

Mark the position of 4 (4, 5, 5) buttonholes evenly spaced along right front edge, bearing in mind that top buttonhole will be worked in the neck-band. With RS facing, pick up the same number of sts along right front edge as for left front edge. Work in Linen st for 6 rows. **Next (buttonhole) row** Cont in Linen st, working a 5-st buttonhole opposite each marker. Work in Linen st for 8 more rows. BO all sts *firmly.*

Neckband

With RS facing, pick up and k150 (168, 186, 204) sts evenly spaced along neck edge. Work in Linen st for 6 rows. **Next (buttonhole) row** Cont in Linen st, working last 5-st buttonhole 4 sts in from right front edge. Work in Linen st for 8 more rows. BO all sts firmly. Sew on buttons opposite buttonholes. With a tapestry needle, weave in loose yarn tails to the WS of work and secure.

Buffalo, aka Bison

Commonly called buffalo, the animals in America are really bison.

In the mid-1800s, there were purportedly 70 million buffalo, but by the end of the century settlers had decimated their number to 1,000. In the late 1800s, William Hornaday of the Smithsonian Institution and others began a vigilant campaign to prevent any further slaughter. By 1905, the National Bison Society had been formed to preserve and protect rangeland for bison. Current estimates place the size of the U.S. herd at 270,000 bison, with most living on private ranches.

Like many other animals, bison have three layers of fiber—with the coarser fibers on the outside and the warm downy fibers on the inside. The guard hairs are hollow and range from 21 to 110 microns in diameter, and the fine downy undercoat hairs are solid and covered with fine scales; these fibers range in diameter from 12 to 29 microns.

Fortunately for knitters, the fiber from these animals is being turned into yarn. Buffalo fiber is strong and insulating, and it's warmer than wool.

As the fiber is not encased in lanolin, it is ideal for those who are allergic to lanolin. Lanolin is also what attracts moths!

Long an emblem of the American plains, if the bison had not been eliminated in such great numbers by the westward-moving settlers, bison fiber would be our native American cashmere!

WOOLY WARREN

TEDDI WHEELER SPECIALIZES IN EXOTIC SPINNING ACCESSORIES. She gets buffalo fiber from a ranch in Missouri, owned by Carol Klein, who has mounted used street sweeper brushes on telephone poles for the buff to scratch against. Otherwise, Teddi would have to use whatever fibers she could find—on barbed wire fences, for example. Carol collects the fiber they have scratched off daily.

Teddi says that buffalo have a multilayered coat with at least three different types of hair: long wiry guard hair, a softer combination of hair that is downy near the skin and straight at the tips (#2), and short hair, about ½ to 1 inch (1.2–2.5cm) long. In the commercial de-hairing process, the #2 hair is removed along with the wiry guard hair, making the percentage of loss quite high. Teddi de-hairs by hand because she has found that the #2 hair is soft enough for garments and that the tips will create a "halo" similar to angora.

At present she creates two buffalo fiber blends: wool, buffalo, and angora; and wool, buffalo, and mohair. She her sells most of her products on Ebay under the name woolywarren.

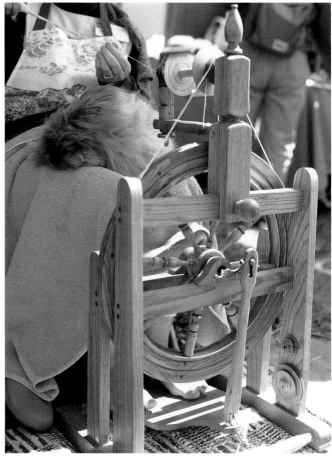

Above left
Angora rabbits not only make fine pets, they are also the source of a fiber that is luxuriously warm and soft.

Above right
Oftentimes the angora rabbit fur can be combed directly from the rabbit and put onto the spinning wheel.

Opposite
Shown is the soft unspun fiber of the angora rabbit and the deliciously soft yarn it spins into.

Bunnies

Everyone is delighted when they see an angora rabbit in the lap of a hand-spinner as she plucks the fibers from the molting rabbit and then spins it into gorgeous yarn. Angora comes from the long-haired domesticated rabbit (not to be confused with the angora goat, which produces mohair).

There are four breeds—Asian, English, French, and German. France and Germany produce most of the commercial angora yarn. In the United States, hand spinners raise the bunnies and produce high-quality angora yarn, while commercial production of angora takes place primarily in Asia. In Nepal, for instance, entire communities have been developed around the mass production of angora.

Fur, which contains both down and stiffer guard hairs, the rabbits can either be combed or clipped. When the fiber is "plucked," it tends to be longer, and so easier for hand spinners to work with, and will not shed as much.

Angora is wonderfully soft, smooth, elegant, silky, and luxurious; however, it is not very elastic. The fiber is very fine—13 to 15 microns—and 1 to 4 inches (2.5–10cm) in length. It is very lightweight and is considered by many to be warmer than wool. When blended with wool, angora will have more structure—and add softness to the wool. Used alone, its inelasticity can create a very saggy item, lightweight but lacking a structured shape.

Angora is great used as a trim around the bottom of sleeves, around the edge of a hat or hood, or as a luxurious trim on the top of a pair of mittens or socks.

The longer fibers tend to shed less. In general, angora yarn tends to be worked up on larger size needles to give the yarn room to loft up a bit. If you have packed an angora garment away and want to fluff it up, use the cold, air-fluff cycle on a dryer to return its loft.

Bodacious Bunny Baby Set

DESIGNED BY SHEILA MEYER

Sheila, a leading sweater designer and owner of One World Button Supply Co., cites her inspiration for this sweater: "It just seemed natural to me that the soft and fuzzy angora/ lambswool blend felt like a bunny rabbit, and what baby wouldn't want one?

Skill Level
Easy

Sizes
Instructions are for infant size 3–6 months. Changes for 9 and 18 months are in parentheses. Shown in size 9 months.

Finished Measurements
Chest 21 (22½, 24)"/53.5 (57, 61)cm

Length 11½ (12½, 14)"/29 (31.5, 35.5)cm

Yarn
ANGEL by Lorna's Laces Hand-Dye Yarns, ½oz/14.25g skeins, each approx 50yd/46m (70% angora/30% lambswool) or a medium weight yarn

Sweater
• 6 (6, 7) skeins in 43NS Sage (MC)

Bunny
• 1 skein in 0NS Natural (CC)

Needles & Notions
Sweater
• One pair each sizes 5 and 7 (3.75 and 4.5mm) needles *or needed to obtain gauge*

• Size 7 (4.5mm) circular needle, 16"/40cm long

• Tapestry needle

Bunny
• One set (4) size 4 (3.5mm) double-pointed needles (dpns) for bunny (**Note:** Short wooden ones work best with the small number of stitches.)

• Two large safety pins for stitch holders

• Stitch marker

• Washable stuffing

• Tapestry needle

Gauge
22 sts and 28 rows = 4"/10cm over St st using larger needles.

Adjust the needle size as necessary to obtain correct gauge.

Construction Notes

SWEATER

1) This sweater is worked in pieces from the bottom up.
2) The neckband is worked in the round after the pieces are assembled.

BUNNY

1) The bunny is worked in small pieces on double pointed needles (dpns).
2) The legs are worked first. They are joined to create the body that is decreased for the neck, then increased for the head.
3) The arms and ears are worked last, then sewn to the body after all pieces are stuffed.

GLOSSARY

⬛ SK2P Slip one st k-wise, k2tog, pass the slipped st over—2 sts decreased.

INSTRUCTIONS FOR THE SWEATER

Back

With smaller needles and MC, CO 58 (62, 66) sts. Work in k2, p2 rib for 1¼"/3 cm, end with a WS row. Change to larger needles and knit across row, inc 0 (2, 4) sts evenly spaced—58 (64, 70) sts. Cont in St st until piece measures 11¼ (12¼, 13½)"/28.5 (31, 34)cm, end with a WS row.

Neck shaping

Next row (RS) Work across first 15 (18, 21) sts, join a 2nd ball of MC and BO center 28 sts for back neck, work to end. Working both sides at the same time, dec 1 st from each neck edge once—14 (17, 20) sts each side. Work even until piece measures 11½ (12½, 14)"/29 (31.5, 35.5)cm from beg. BO all sts each side.

Front

Work as for back until piece measures 9¾ (10¾, 11¾)"/24.5 (27.5, 30)cm from beg, end with a WS row.

Neck shaping

Next row (RS) Work across first 19 (22, 25) sts, join a 2nd skein of MC and BO center 20 sts for front neck, work to end. Working both sides at the same time, BO 3 sts from each neck once, then 2 sts once—14 (17, 20) sts each side. Work even until piece measures same length as back to shoulder. BO all sts each side.

Sleeves

With smaller needles and MC, CO 26 (30, 38) sts. Work in k2, p2 rib for 1¼"/3cm. Change to larger needles. Cont in St st and inc 1 st each side every 4th row 4 (4, 8) times, then every 6th row 4 (4, 5) times—42 (46, 64) sts. Work even until piece measures 7½ (8½, 10)"/19 (21.5, 25.5)cm from beg or desired length. BO all sts.

Pocket

With larger needles and MC, CO 22 sts. Work in St st for 2½"/6.5. BO all sts.

FINISHING

Block pieces gently to avoid felting the angora. Sew shoulder seams.

Neckband

With RS facing, circular needle and MC, pick up and k 86 (86, 90) sts evenly spaced around neck edge. Work around in k2, p2 rib for ¾"/2cm. BO all sts loosely in rib.

Place markers 3¾ (4¼, 5¾)"/9.5 (10.5, 14.5)cm down from shoulders on back and front. Sew sleeves to armholes between markers. Sew side and sleeve seams. Center pocket on front, then sew in place. Using CC, stitch rolled top edge down, using blanket stitch or overcast stitch. With a tapestry needle, weave in loose yarn tails to the WS of work and secure.

INSTRUCTIONS FOR THE BUNNY

Legs

With dpns, CO 6 sts. Divide sts evenly between 3 needles (2 sts on each needle). Join and pm to indicate beg of rnd. Knit 1 rnd.
Next rnd K1 into front and back of each stitch around—12 sts. Cont around in St st for 15 rnds. Place 6 sts on one safety pin and 6 sts on 2nd safety pin. Work 2nd leg as for first; leave sts on needles.

Body

Arrange 24 sts from legs in a circle on 3 dpns (8 sts on each). Join and pm to indicate beg of rnd. Work even in St st for 8 rnds.

Separate for armholes

Transfer front 12 sts to one needle and work back and forth in St st for 6 rows. BO 3 sts each side. Place rem 6 sts on safety pin. Rep from * to * for the 12 back sts—6 sts; leave sts on needle.

Neck and head

Arrange rem 12 sts from body on 3 dpns (4 sts on each). Work 5 rnds (neck), then inc 1 st at each end of each needle (beg of head)—18 sts. Knit 7 rnds.
Next (dec) rnd [K2tog] 9 times—9 sts.
Next (dec) rnd [K2tog, k1] 3 times—6 sts. BO all sts.

Arms

With dpns, CO 6 sts (2 sts on each needle). Join and pm to indicate beg of rnd. Knit 10 rnds. Bind off all sts.

Ears

With dpns, CO 3 sts. Work back and forth in St st for 2 rows.
Next row Inc 1 st each side—5 sts. Work 8 rows even.
Next row SK2P—3 sts. Purl one row.
Next row SK2P—1 st. Fasten off.

FINISHING

Close small opening between legs with tail. Stuff legs, body, head and arms. Sew each "hand" opening closed, then sew open end of arms to armholes. Sew on ears approx ¾"/2cm below top of head. With a tapestry needle, run loose yarn tails inside body.

Embroidery

With MC, embroider face, then duplicate stitch or embroider heart.

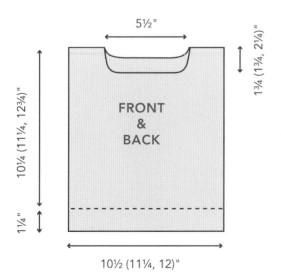

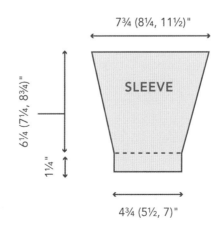

LORNA'S LACES

IN 2003, BETH CASEY PURCHASED LORNA'S LACES Hand-Dyed Yarn from its original owner, Lorna Miser. After establishing this wonderful company, Lorna decided to return to her first love: designing. Beth had been working in the corporate world and needed a change, and became proprietor of Lorna's Laces after answering a classified ad in the back of a knitting magazine.

The hallmark of Lorna's Laces has always been beautiful, clear colors in classic fibers. Working exclusviely with animal fibers (like wool, mohair, angora, and silk), the centerpiece of their offerings is their Shepard line, a series of four superwash merino yarns that are milled exclusively for Lorna's Laces. This extraordinarily soft, luscious yarn comes in sock, sport, worsted, and bulky weights.

"I'm often asked where we come up with the ideas for our colors," Beth Casey says. "The simple answer is everywhere. The Glenwood colorway came about onefall evening when I walked by a terra cotta pot filled with yellow and orange mums. Tahoe came to me while shopping in a department store's towel display and pondering which colors would look nice together. I think it's a matter of keeping my eyes open and looking for beautiful colors everywhere."

Silk

A fiber in a class all its own, silk has been used in the manufacture of exquisite and luxurious textiles for centuries. The intricate process of cultivating the fiber of the silkworm produces a fabric that is lightweight yet warm, drapes well, and is highly receptive to dyeing, producing a richness rarely seen in other textiles.

The ancient art of turning the silkworms into fiber for spinning is called sericulture and dates back to around 2700 BC. Sericulture is the cultivation of the insect through the stages from egg to caterpillar to cocoon, and the cultivation of the mulberry trees that grow the leaves on which the silkworms feed.

As a Chinese legend tells the story, the reigning prince, Hoang-Li, presented his wife Si-ling-chi with the challenge of determining how the thread from the silkworm cocoon could be manufactured into a thread and woven into fabric. After discovering how best to raise the silkworm and how to reel the silk for use in fabric production, she was named the "Goddess of Silk Worms."

This process became one of the most closely guarded secrets in Chinese history. Near the beginning of the second century BC, travel began along the 4,000-mile (6,435km) Silk Road—the trade route linking China with the West—not

The Silkworm and Its Silk

There are many kinds of silkworms, each creating a silk fiber unique unto itself. Most common is the *Bombyx mori*, which feeds on the leaves of the mulberry tree—*morus* meaning "mulberry" in Latin. The fibers produced by the cocoon fibers are soft to the touch, brilliantly white, and unusually fine, belying the amazingly strong quality of the silk fiber. This fine, bright fiber lends itself well to accepting dye, presenting color that is bright and lustrous. All these qualities make it ideal for commercial production.

Wild silk fibers, however, are also used for commercial production in much smaller quantities. Produced by wild silkworms of the saturniid moth family, they are hand-picked from trees and shrubs. Tussah silkworms, for instance, which feed on all kinds of trees with leaves that are rich in tannins, produce fibers that range from brown to golden in color. Muga silkworms produce a creamy golden or creamy white silk. Although stronger than Bombyx mori fibers, the darker color of wild silk produces a fiber that is deep and rich in color when naturally dyed. These fibers, which are typically cultivated regionally, are stronger than those of the Bombyx mori.

only carrying ideology and religion between the two civilizations, but cargo as well. From the west came wool, gold and silver, and from the east (China) came silk and jade.

China, the source of all silk at the time, kept the secret of its sericulture closely guarded and intact until shortly after AD 300, when it leaked its way into India. As legend has it, the egg of the silkworm and the seed of the mulberry tree were smuggled westward into India concealed in the headdress of a Chinese princess.

Not long thereafter, in AD 552, the Byzantine emperor Justinian sent two Persian monks on an excursion to China. They brought the secrets of sericulture to the Roman Empire when they successfully smuggled a supply of silkworm eggs hidden inside hollow canes back into Constantinople, which soon grew to become the leading center of the silk trade in the West.

Today, China continues to be the world's leading producer and exporter of silk, followed by Japan. The two countries manufacture more than 50 percent of the world production. While silk accounts for less than 1 percent of world fiber

Left
The stages of silk: Silkworms feed on mulberry leaves and then spin a cocoon. The cocoons are then unwound to make silk or the moth is allowed to escape and the cocoons are degummed and spun like other fibers. Shown here (clockwise, from middle left) are Peace Silk cocoons; "Muga" cocoons from India; Peace Silk Moths; spun silk; and degummed Peace Silk cocoons.

Considered an animal fiber, silk is produced by the silkworm—which is not really a worm at all, but a caterpillar that spins a cocoon for protection as it changes from a caterpillar into a moth.

production, it is an attractive industry in countries where labor costs are low, as the labor required for end-production is intensive.

Cultivating silkworms is an intricate and intriguing process that begins with the cultivator of the silkworm eggs. This person is the careful breeder of the moths and administers the egg-laying process—a substantial job in that each moth lays 300 to 500 pinhead-size eggs. The moth then dies days later.

The eggs are sold to farmers who raise the silkworm from egg stage to cocoon. Eggs are stored at a low temperature in order to develop. They are then exposed to warm temperatures (80°F) for an incubation period of 10 days, at which time they hatch. One ounce of eggs will produce between 40,000 and 60,000 silkworms!

For nearly a month, the larvae feed on mulberry leaves, which are also grown by the farmer. In order to produce two pounds of raw silk, roughly 485 pounds (220kg) of mulberry leaves are required!

"Ripe" silkworms are then ready to create a cocoon. Two silk glands extrude filaments made of the protein fibroin; the silkworm creates the cocoon by manufacturing and encasing itself with this continuous fiber. A second pair of glands produce sericin, a substance that bonds the filaments together. A double silk filament is extruded via the spinneret located in the silkworm's head. One cocoon can produce up to 13,000 feet (3,962m) of filament as it adds layer upon layer of fiber.

Once the cocoon is complete, the silkworm metamorphoses into a chrysalis and then a moth. The newborn moths do not eat or fly; rather, they lay eggs and die. And the process begins again.

Adult moths extrude a fluid/spit which dissolves the silk cocoon, allowing the moth to push its way out of the cocoon. Silkworm farmers, on the other hand, kill the moths before they emerge by baking the cocoon—and the moth in a hot oven. The cocoon is then soaked in boiling water to loosen the thread so that it is ready to be wound onto a bobbin.

The remaining cocoons are then sold to reeling mills, which soak the cocoons to soften the sericin before the silk fiber is unwound. Several cocoons are unwound simultaneously to create a thicker strand, which is wound onto a reel and dried. The reeled silk is then twisted together into yarns in a process called throwing. (The thickness of the yarn is measured in "denier"—the weight in grams; finer silk has a lower denier.) The raw silk is then boiled in order to remove the gummy sericin remaining; this process is called degumming, and leaves the silk lustrous and supple.

Waste silk, which is just silk that is not suitable for reeling, is carded and combed instead, in a process similar to that used to produce the "beast" fibers. This waste silk is used to make silk tops that are then spun into silk yarn.

Opposite, above left
Hanging from a "butterfly" hook, these balls of silk chenille yarn show off the different textures found in the silk.

Opposite, above right
Some more unique fibers include paper-wrapped silk; natural undyed silk; and bamboo (a member of the plant family of fibers).

Opposite, below left
Silk fiber blends beautifully, lending luster to any blended yarn. Here it is shown blended with cashmere.

Opposite, below right
Several skeins show the natural beauty of plant-dyed silk.

AURORA SILK AND THE LOGWOOD PROJECT

AURORA SILK, BUILT ON EXPERT OWNER, ARTISAN, AND MASTER DYER CHERYL KOLANDERS'S KNOWLEDGE
of dyeing and silk, is a resource not to be overlooked by the natural dyer and silk enthusiast. Not only does Aurora Silk offer silk for spinning along with a palette of silk yarns for knitting, it is also a source of kits for raising your own silkworms.

Cheryl has aligned her company with the Logwood Project, based in the Dominican Republic. At the outset, it was simply an effort to bring in logwood dyestuff for the needs of her natural dye studio. It has since evolved into an indigenous support and economic development project. In addition to logwood dyestuff, the raising of Peace Silk (silkworms) has begun. (Peace Silk is made by allowing the moth to emerge from the cocoon before spinning the silk—as opposed to boiling the cocoon whole, as is done in commercial processing of silk.)

Community benefits that have been achieved through the Logwood Project include water lines, drinkable water, a bridge, school supplies, musical instruments, a library of both Spanish and English books, and a clinic dispensing natural medicines.

The Uma Sweater

DESIGNED BY VICKI SQUARE

Vicki reports that the deep U-neckline of this elegant silk sweater begged for a name that began with "U." A fan of both the name Uma and the beautiful contemporary actor, she thought the name was a perfect choice for the sweater.

Vicki took the concept of the plain pullover and knit it in slimming and fun-to-knit side-to-side garter stitch. The textural silk yarn from Muench in this flattering shade of cranberry is especially lovely. While it doesn't show in the photograph, Vicki offers the option of having a longer back panel if you want, or you can make the sweater the same length all around.

Skill Level
Easy

Sizes
Instructions are for Small. Changes for Medium and Large are in parentheses. Shown in size Small.

Finished Measurements
Bust 38 (42, 46)"/96.5 (106.5, 117)cm

Front length 19 (20, 21)"/48 (51, 53.5)cm (after blocking)

Back length 23 (24, 25)"/58.5 (61, 63.5)cm (after blocking)

Yarn
SIR GALLI by Muench Yarns, 1¾oz/50g balls, each approx 104yd/95m (100% silk) or a medium weight yarn

• 11 (12, 13) balls in #4912 Cranberry

Needles & Notions
• One pair size 7 (4.5mm) needles *or size needed to obtain gauge*

• Split markers or safety pins

• Tapestry needle

Gauge
17 sts and 32 rows (16 ridges) = 4"/10cm in garter st using size 7 (4.5mm) needles.

Adjust the needle size as necessary to obtain correct gauge.

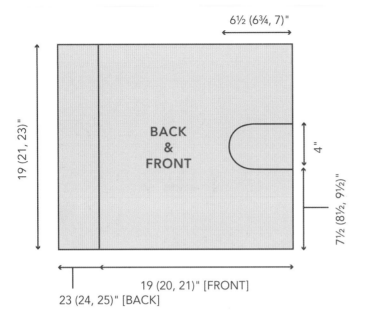

6½ (6¾, 7)"

BACK & FRONT

19 (21, 23)"

4"

7½ (8½, 9½)"

19 (20, 21)" [FRONT]

23 (24, 25)" [BACK]

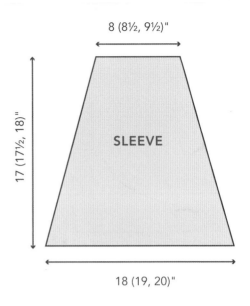

8 (8½, 9½)"

SLEEVE

17 (17½, 18)"

18 (19, 20)"

Construction Notes

1) The back and front of this garment are worked sideways in garter stitch (the ridges run lengthwise).
2) The back is longer than the front. The knitted fabric will relax after blocking and will measure slightly longer than preblocking.
3) After the shoulders are invisibly seamed, the sleeve stitches are picked up and worked down to the cuff.

GLOSSARY

※ **Lifted inc** Lift up the garter st bar in the row below and place on the left-hand needle; knit into the back of the loop.

※ **Cable cast-on** Insert the right-hand needle *between* the last two stitches on the left-hand needle; wrap yarn around the needle k-wise, pull through and place resulting loop on left-hand needle. Repeat for the indicated number of cast-on stitches required.

※ **Invisible seaming for garter stitch** With RS facing and using a blunt-end tapestry needle and garment yarn, catch a lower garter ridge loop on the right piece and pull yarn through. Cross to the left piece and catch an upper garter ridge loop and pull yarn through. (**Note:** The lower loop on the right side will not be right at the edge of the fabric.) Pull thread firmly to neaten edge, but not so tightly that the seam is no longer flexible.

INSTRUCTIONS FOR THE SWEATER

Back

CO 94 (99, 104) sts; tail marks lower left back corner. Work in garter st until piece measures 19 (21, 23)"/48 (53.5, 58.5)cm from beg, end with a RS row. BO all sts loosely.

Front

CO 80 (85, 90) sts; tail marks lower right front corner. Work in garter st until piece measures 7½ (8½, 9½)"/19 (21.5, 24)cm from beg, end with a RS row.

Neck shaping

Next row (WS) BO first 23 (24, 25) sts, knit to end.
*****Next row** Knit to last 3 sts, k2tog, k1.
Next row Wyif, slip 1 st p-wise, yarn back, knit to end. Rep from * 4 times more—52 (56, 60) sts. Cont to slip first st at neck edge p-wise and work even until piece measures 10 (11, 12)"/25.5 (28, 30.5)cm from beg, end with a WS row.
******Next row** Knit.
Next row Wyif, slip 1 st p-wise, work a lifted inc, then knit to end. Rep from ** 4 times more.
Next row (RS) Knit to end, turn. Cable cast-on 23 (24, 25) sts. Work even until shoulder measures same as opposite shoulder; piece should measure 19 (21, 23)"/48 (53.5, 58.5)cm from beg, end with a RS row. BO all sts.

MUENCH YARNS

was inspired to start her company in the 1980s after finding the yarn selection in her San Francisco community a dissapointment. Working together with the European manufacturers, she began importing yarns into the United States via her company, Muench Yarns. As her son Marcus describes it, "Lots of small business sucess stories start in someone's garage. I remember everything starting very slowly in the living room: the garage was step two for Muench Yarns."

Although Dieta passed away in 1991, the company continues to operate under the leadership of her family members and has grown to be one of the larger yarn companies, offering quality yarns, needles, buttons, and accessories.

Muench Yarns prides itself on its involvement with the community through philanthropic efforts, aligning itself with such causes as Knit For Her Cure™, which encourages yarn lovers to join in the fight against women's cancers, and Operation Toasty Toes, which provides knitted socks for U.S. service men and women stationed throughout the world, as well as by regularly donating yarns and needles to support the teaching of arts and crafts in schools.

Sleeves

With RS facing, seam shoulders invisibly working from ridge to ridge. Place split ring or safety pin markers 9 (9½, 10)"/23 (24, 25.5)cm from shoulder seam on both back and front. With RS facing, pick up and knit 76 (80, 84) sts evenly spaced along armhole edge between markers. Work in garter stitch for 6 (2, 2) rows.

Dec row K1, ssk, knit to last 3 sts, k2tog, k1. Rep dec row every 6th row 20 (21, 21) times more—34 (36, 38) sts. Work even until sleeve measures 17 (17½, 18)"/43 (44.5, 45.5)cm, end with RS row. BO all sts loosely.

FINISHING

Block pieces to measurements using wet-towel method. Let dry completely. With RS facing, seam the sleeves invisibly. Whipstitch or overcast side seams, working from underarm down, leaving the last 1"/2.5cm of front unseamed for flap; the back will have a 5"/12.5cm flap. With a tapestry needle, weave in loose yarn tails to the WS of work and secure.

Chapter 3
PLANTS

When pondering the range of plant fibers and sources, it's a wonder how the world's varied cultures all recognized the viability of plants indigenous to their area as a source of fiber and, ultimately, clothing. While cotton might appear an obvious choice for a spinning fiber, the process involved in making linen fiber from flax is a complex one. And it's a further jump to fathom that pineapple leaves or agave plants produce more

than just pineapples and tequila, respectively. Cheers to our brilliant fiber forefathers and foremothers! Plant fibers are made from cellulose, the primary structural component in the cell wall of plants. Clothes made from plant fibers are known to keep the wearer cool. They tend to be rather sturdy, but they will stretch out. While plant fibers cannot be made to do what they truly are not able to do, you can blend them with other fibers to add the quality that you are looking for, whether it be shine, elasticity, or warmth.

Cotton

Cotton is the most widely used of any fiber. The earliest known place where cotton was cultivated is India, and the oldest fragment of cotton textile dates to about 3000 BC. Some of these fine Indian cottons were spun of fibers from a species of cotton that was so fine, the fabrics were transparent. Fine Indian cottons were among the items that Christopher Columbus was seeking on his first voyage, and interestingly, he found people in South America wearing it. It is speculated that cotton migrated from Asia with the earliest inhabitants of the Americas, which would make cultivating cotton very old indeed.

Cotton grows best in hot, dry climates, including the southern United States, South America, Egypt, China, and Russia.

As a cotton plant grows, it first produces a flower, then a pod containing a mass of cotton fibers surrounding the seeds. When the pod opens, the cotton is picked and passed through a cotton gin that removes the seeds and the short fibers, called linters. The cotton fiber varies in length (from 3/8" to 2¼" [1–6cm]) and color (from green to white to brown), depending on the type of plant.

Interestingly, cotton that is naturally colored green or brown will get darker as it is washed. The green cotton used in the chenille robe shown on page 124 was boiled before it was skeined and it is a much different color than the green in the poncho shown on page 121. However, when it was growing on the plant, all the cotton started out pretty much the same color.

Cotton is stronger than rayon or wool and weaker than silk or linen. Mercerized cotton has been treated with an alkali that causes the cotton to swell and straighten and look more lustrous.

Commercially, cotton has typically required the use of a lot of pesticides during cultivation. According to the Sustainable Cotton Project, it takes 17 teaspoons of synthetic fertilizers plus ¾ teaspoon of pesticides and herbicides to raise 9 ounces (255g) of cotton—enough for one T-shirt. Buying organic cotton shows that you are making a commitment to using fewer pesticides in the world. As the demand for organic cotton has gone up, there is more and more of it available, both for hand-knitters and for people who want to wear organic cotton clothes.

Opposite
Naturally color-grown cotton comes from the cotton plant in a wide variety of shades, as illustrated by the array of colors in these samples.

Lilliana's Organic Cotton Poncho and Drawstring Pouch

DESIGNED BY BARBARA ALBRIGHT

Natural-colored organic cotton from Peru was used to make this very, very soft poncho. It is a perfect choice for children who complain about itchy fabric around their necks, as this yarn feels like butter. You can make this easy poncho design in other medium-weight yarns as well. The coordinating drawstring pouch with its ruffled top is perfectly suited for carrying seashells, acorns, rocks, or other nature-walk finds.

Skill Level
Easy

Sizes
Instructions are for children's size 3–6. Changes for 6–9 and 9–12 are in parentheses. Shown in size 3–6.

Finished Measurements
Poncho
Neck circumference 14 (15, 16)"/35.5 (38, 40.5)cm

Circumference at lower edge approx 112 (128, 144)"/280 (325, 360)cm

Length from base of neck to one of the points approx 18 (21, 24)"/46 (53.5, 61)cm

Drawstring pouch
3" x 5"/7.5 x 12.5cm

Yarn
INCA COTTON by Henry's Attic, 8oz/227g skeins, each approx 325yd/297m (100% organic cotton, undyed natural plant color) or a medium weight yarn

• 1 skein in Oz (A)

• 1 skein in Ecru (B)

Needles & Notions
Poncho
• Size 8 (5mm) circular needles, 16"/40, 24"/60cm and 32"/80cm long *or size needed to obtain gauge*

• Size 6 (4mm) circular needle, 16"/40cm long

• Four stitch markers, one in a different color

• Tapestry needle

Pouch
• One set (4) size 8 (5mm) double-pointed needles (dpns)

• Size H/8 (5mm) crochet hook

• Tapestry needle

Gauge
16 sts and 25 rnds = 4"/10 cm in St st using larger circular needle.

Adjust the needle size if necessary to obtain the correct gauge.

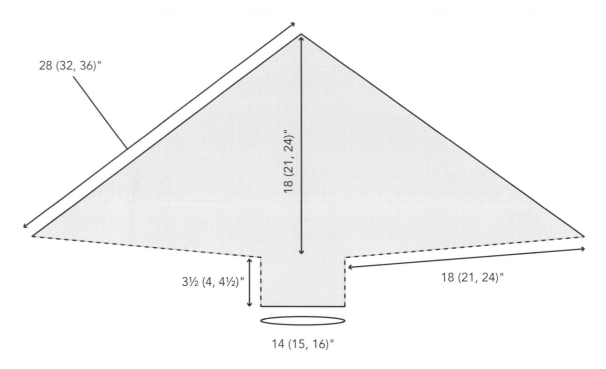

28 (32, 36)"

18 (21, 24)"

3½ (4, 4½)"

18 (21, 24)"

14 (15, 16)"

Construction Notes

Poncho

1) The poncho is worked in the round from the ribbed neck down to the striped body (which is shaped by increasing on every other round), ending with a striped garter ridge border.

2) The length can be adjusted by knitting more (or fewer) rounds as desired.

Pouch

The pouch is worked in the round from the bottom up, ending with eyelets through which a crocheted drawstring will pass.

GLOSSARY

▨ **M1L** Insert the left needle under the running thread between the needles from front to back and knit into the back loop.

▨ **M1R** Insert the left needle under the running thread between the needles from back to front and knit into the front loop.

INSTRUCTIONS FOR THE PONCHO

Beg at neck edge, with smaller needle and A, CO 76 (80, 84) sts. Join, taking care not to twist sts on needle. Pm to indicate beg of rnd and sl marker every rnd. Work around in k1, p1 rib for 3½ (4, 4½)"/9 (10, 11.5)cm.

Next rnd Using 3 markers in a different color than beg of rnd marker, work as foll: *k19 (20, 21), pm; rep from * around twice more, end k19 (20, 21). Change to larger, shortest needle. Cont in St st and stripe pat as folls:

Rnds 1, 3, 5, and 7 (Inc rnd) *Sm, M1L, knit to 1 st before next marker, M1R, k1; rep from * around—27 (28, 29) sts between markers at end of Rnd 7.

Rnds 2, 4, and 6 Knit.

Cont in garter st (changing to longer needle when needed) as folls:

Rnds 8, 10, 12, and 14 Purl.

Rnd 9 With B, rep Inc rnd—29 (30, 31) sts between markers.

Rnd 11 With A, rep Inc rnd—31 (32, 33) sts between markers.

Rnd 13 With B, rep Inc rnd—33 (34, 35) sts between markers.

Rnd 15 With A, rep Inc rnd—35 (36, 37) sts between markers.

Rnd 16 Purl. Cont to rep Inc rnd every other rnd and work 7-rnd St st stripes, beg with A and alternating colors, until there are 5 (6, 7) stripes in A after the garter ridges.

Next 8 rnds Rep Rnds 8–15. BO all sts p-wise.

FINISHING

Block lightly to measurements. With a tapestry

needle, weave in loose yarn tails to WS of work and secure.

INSTRUCTIONS FOR THE DRAWSTRING POUCH

With dpns and A, CO 24 sts. Divide sts evenly between 3 needles (8 sts on each). Join, taking care not to twist sts on needle. Pm to indicate beg of rnd and sl marker every rnd. Knit 12 rnds, then purl 1 rnd. Cont in stripe pat as folls: *With B, knit 1 rnd then purl 1 rnd. With A, knit 1 rnd then purl 1 rnd; rep from * once more. With A only, knit next 8 rnds.

Next (eyelet) rnd *K3, yo; rep from * around—32 sts.

Next rnd K1 in front and back of each st around—64 sts. BO all sts.

FINISHING

With crochet hook and A and B held tog, crochet a 22"/56cm chain for drawstring. Fasten off. Weave the drawstring in and out of the eyelets around top of pouch. Using a tapestry needle, weave in the yarn tails on the drawstring and the loose yarn tails to WS of pouch and secure. Thread tapestry needle with a 18"/46cm length of A and sew bottom of bag together. Tie ends of drawstring together with an overhand knot.

HENRY'S ATTIC

LOCATED IN MONROE, NEW YORK, HENRY'S ATTIC aims to find yarns from around the world and sell them to retailers. Some of those retailers dye these yarns, so you may be correct when you note that the same yarns from two different sources look identical. Henry's Attic also offers consummate fiber lovers the opportunity to design their own yarn, using a range of fibers and yarns.

Crochet Techniques

Even if you never plan to crochet a granny square, knowing the following crochet techniques will lend a polished look to your knitted treasures.

CROCHET CHAIN

- Make a slipknot and place it on a crochet hook.
- *Bring the yarn over the hook as shown and draw it through the slipknot; repeat from * as many times as necessary. (Illus. 1)
- To finish off a crochet chain, cut the yarn and bring the yarn tail through the last loop on the crochet hook. Pull the yarn tail to tighten and secure.

SINGLE CROCHET

- Insert the hook into a stitch and bring the yarn over the hook from back to front and to the back again (a yarn over the hook); draw a loop through the stitch—(2 loops on hook). (Illus. 2)
- Yarn over the hook, and pull through both loops on the hook—(1 loop on hook). (Illus. 3)
- Move to the next stitch and repeat instructions from beginning.

1

2

3

Chenille in the Morning

DESIGNED BY VALENTINA DEVINE

Mornings are much more civilized when you have a snuggly robe to cuddle up in. Valentina Devine's cotton chenille robe is made of organic cotton chenille from Vreseis. Valentina has added her own special touch by embellishing the robe's pocket with a handful of buttons from her "button jar."

Skill Level
Easy

Sizes
Instructions are for one size fits Small to Large (10–16). See construction notes for sizing up or down.

Finished Measurements
Bust 53"/134.5cm

Length 46"/117cm

Yarn
FOXFIBRE® BOILED COTTON CHENILLE by Vreseis Ltd., 16oz/453.3g skeins, each 600yd/548.5m (100% organic, undyed cotton) or a super bulky weight yarn

• 64oz/1814g in Green

Needles & Notions
• One pair size 15 (10mm) needles *or size needed to obtain gauge*

• Size J/10 (6mm) crochet hook

• Stitch holders or waste yarn

• Tapestry needle

• Small amount of crochet cotton or embroidery floss

• Assorted buttons

Gauge
17-st strip = 9"/23cm over seed st using size 15 (10mm) needles.

Adjust the needle size as necessary to obtain correct gauge.

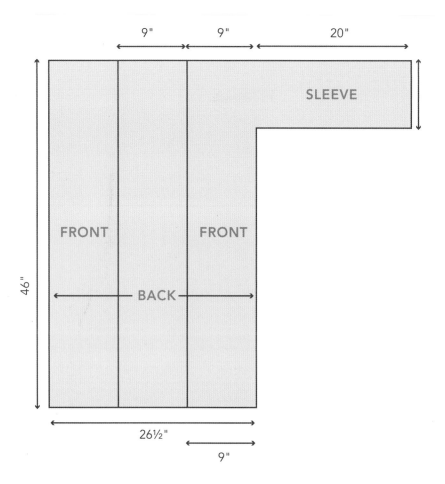

Construction Notes

1) This garment is knitted in individual strips.

2) Each strip is the same width.

3) If you would like to adjust the size, simply cast on more (or fewer) stitches per strip to fit the size you need.

4) Due to the weight of the fabric, this garment will stretch. Bearing this in mind, you may want to work strips about 4"/10cm shorter than your desired finished length.

Designer's Hint

To get an attractive edge, which makes it easier to sew or crochet the strips together, an edge stitch is recommended. To do the edge stitch, slip the last stitch on every row as if to purl and knit the firststitch of every row through the back loop.

GLOSSARY

▨ **3-needle bindoff** Holding needles parallel with RS together and WS facing, knit 1 each from front and back needles together, *k2tog from front and back needles and pass the first st over the second to bind off; rep from * to end.

INSTRUCTIONS FOR THE COAT

Seed stitch

(over an odd number of sts)

Row 1 K1, *p1, k1; rep from * to end.

Rep Row 1 for seed st.

The strip

CO 17 sts. Work in seed st until strip measures stated length for each piece.

Back

Make 3 strips 46"/117cm long or desired length. Do not BO; put on holder or waste yarn. Sew or slip stitch crochet the back strips tog.

Fronts

Make 2 strips the same length as back and using 3-needle bindoff, join each to one of the back shoulder strips.

VRESEIS LIMITED, BY SALLY VRESEIS FOX

WHEN IT COMES TO ORGANIC COTTON, SALLY FOX IS REVERED FOR HER EFFORTS IN BRINGING organic colored cotton to the forefront in America. A knitter and spinner since she was twelve, Sally taught handspinning as a way to earn money during college.

Sally received her master's in integrated pest management (a program that taught sustainable agriculture techniques) at the University of California in Riverside. Her first job was as a cotton breeder, and while she did not especially like the job, she was enchanted by the natural brown color of the cotton. Because the fiber of the cotton was too short for handspinning, she started to breed the cotton to have longer staples by combining the longest white cotton with the short brown fibers. Not only was the yarn that resulted from this cross-bred cotton good for hand-spinning, it could be spun on machines as well.

During her second year of breeding in 1984, Sally created her business, Vreseis. In addition to growing her own cotton, she began educating farmers on how to produce cotton organically.

Generally, farmers are given technical specifications on what kind of cotton is wanted. Because they get more money for more volume, farmers will tend to select those plants that give the highest yield— and produce the working-horse cotton of the world. The easiest way to get the highest yield is to breed for thick fiber, which feels harsher. Chemists then soften this coarser and harsher cotton by using enzymes or abrasives such as lava, stone, or gravel.

By contrast, Sally's goal is to breed for fineness, and she says that her green cotton is finer than cashmere (see bottom left photo on page 128). Sea island cotton is a famous white cotton that is both strong and fine. Sally got some sea island cotton seeds from a seed bank, crossed the green cotton with the sea island cotton, and produced her lovely fine green cotton.

Shawl collar

Make 1 strip twice the length of the front strips, plus approx 6"/15cm for the back neck as folls: knit until you think it is ALMOST long enough. Keeping the sts on the needle, beg attaching the collar strip to the right front, back neck edge and down the left front. This way you do not have to constantly measure the shawl collar strip; just add as many rows as needed as you are attaching the strip.

Sleeves

Make 4 strips (2 for each sleeve) 20"/51cm long or desired length.

Pocket

CO 17 sts. Work in seed st until you have a square. BO in seed st.

FINISHING

Find the center of each sleeve and pin to the shoulder center seam. Attach sleeves. Turn back bottom edge of sleeves for cuffs and anchor in place. Sew side seams. With a tapestry needle, weave in loose yarn tails to the WS of work and secure.

Pocket edging

With RS facing and crochet hook, join yarn with a sl st in any corner. **Rnd 1** Ch-1, making sure that work lies flat, sc evenly around, working 2 sc in each corner. Join rnd with a sl st in first sc. **Rnd 2** Ch-1, working in the opposite direction, work rev sc (also known as Crab st) in each st around. Join rnd with a sl st in first sc. Fasten off. Sew decorative buttons on pocket as desired. Using a crochet cotton or embroidery floss, sew pocket on right front as shown.

Belt

With crochet hook and 2 strands of yarn held tog, crochet a chain to desired length. Fasten off. Double knot the ends.

Linen

The bast fiber family includes linen from flax, jute, hemp, and ramie. What distinguishes it from other plant fibers is that the fiber comes from the inner bark tissue of the stems of the source plant. The overall height of the plant determines the length of the fiber.

Just like Sleeping Beauty, most of us would be enchanted that sinewy flax can be spun into cool, beautiful linen fibers. Flax is the oldest textile in the world. Its earliest known use dates from 8000 BC. Pharaohs in Egyptian tombs were frequently wrapped in linen fabrics. People report sleeping better between two pure linen sheets and artists frequently use this sturdy fiber to make their canvases. Some types of paper are made from the linen fiber as well.

Environmentally, flax is a good crop to grow, as it requires very little fertilizing. In addition to producing fiber, flax produces flax oil, which is used in soaps, cosmetics, paints, and printing inks.

There are two types of flax plants. One type is grown for its seeds, which are a good source of omega-3 fatty acids. The other type of flax plant, which grows to about 30 to 47 inches (76–119cm), is cultivated for its fiber. It has a short growing season of about 100 days. At that time, the plant is pulled up out of the ground and dried in a sunny location.

First the dried plants are pulled through rippling combs—wooden or iron devices with several rows of upright nails—to remove the seeds. This is known as *rippling*. Next the flax is *retted*: It is soaked to loosen the fibrous straw in the core of the plant from the outer plant layer where the flax fibers are found. Flax is retted either by being laid out on the ground and letting the dew wet it, or by being weighted down and submerged in water. The fibers are then dried and scutched: The woody parts and bark are removed through a

crushing motion that frees up the fibers. Then the fibers are spun into yarn.

Linen is a very strong fiber, but it is not very soft. If you want to knit with a softer linen fiber, some recommend that you wash the fiber before working with it. Because it is made of cellulose and pectin, linen will grow softer with washing as the pectin washes away. Others suggest that you iron the fabric after it is created to make it softer. Linen is a fiber that can take abuse and will get softer for it! Like other plant/cellulose fibers, linen does not have a lot of stretch, so ribbing does not pull it in as it does other fibers.

Linen maintains its structure and is a good choice for blending with a softer fiber that has some bounce to it.

Above
The unspun fibers of Soy Silk, Ingeo, and Bamboo are as soft as they are strong.

Opposite, above left
Undyed linen.

Opposite, above right
Plant-dyed linen.

Opposite, below left
Naturally colored cotton yarn, like this chenille yarn, will grow darker the more it is washed. The colors are an integral part of the fiber, not a dye. The darker one has been washed.

Opposite, below right
Creating linen yarn starts with flaxseed, which produces the flax plant. The outer layers of the plant stalk make up flax strick, which is spun into linen fiber.

Memories of Ukraine

DESIGNED BY LIDIA KARABINICH

Lidia prefers to knit with natural fibers and especially loves linen because it softens with every wash. For·her, linen brings back childhood memories of the flax fields near her grandmother's home in Ukraine. She remembers seeing them flowering with tiny blue blossoms. As with many of her sweaters, Lidia started this one with her signature seamless yoke and there is no sewing to do when you are finished!

Skill Level
Intermediate

Sizes
Instructions are for Small. Changes for Medium, Large, and X-Large are in parentheses. Shown in size Small.

Finished Measurements
Bust 33½ (36½, 39¼, 42)"/85 (92.5, 99.5, 106.5)cm

Length 22½ (23½, 25, 25)"/57 (59.5, 63.5, 63.5)cm

Yarn
EUROFLAX ORIGINALS by Louet Sales, 1¾oz/50g skeins, each approx 135yd/123.5m (100% linen) or a fine weight yarn

• 8 (9, 11, 12) skeins in Champagne

Needles & Notions
• Size 4 (3.5mm) circular needles, 16"/40cm and 24"/60cm long *or size needed to obtain gauge*

• Stitch holders or waste yarn

• Stitch marker

Gauge
20 sts and 29 rnds = 4"/10cm over lace pat using size 4 (3.5mm) needle (after blocking)

Adjust the needle size as necessary to obtain correct gauge.

Gauge Swatch
CO 30 sts. Cont as folls: p2, *work 5-st lace panel, p2; rep from * to end. Work 2 reps of chart. BO all sts. Block before measuring gauge.

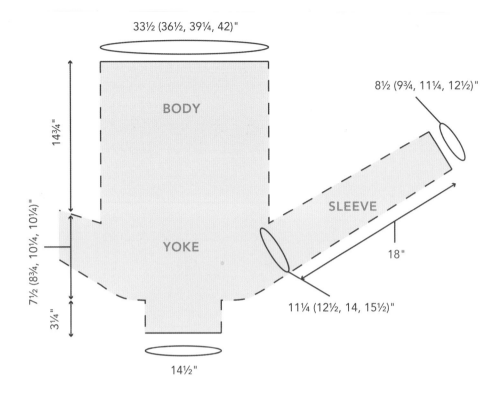

33½ (36½, 39¼, 42)"

BODY

14¾"

8½ (9¾, 11¼, 12½)"

SLEEVE

18"

7½ (8¾, 10¼, 10¼)"

3¼"

YOKE

11¼ (12½, 14, 15½)"

14½"

Construction Notes

1) *This close-fitting pullover is worked in the round from the neck down.*

2) *The yoke is increased by inserting additional lace panels over 6 (8, 7) rnds.*

3) *When the yoke is done, stitches are placed on holders or waste yarn for sleeves, which will be worked after the body is completed.*

4) *This sweater requires no seaming.*

GLOSSARY

▩ **M1 p-wise** Insert LH needle under the horizontal thread between the stitch just worked and the next st and p into the back of it.

5LP 5-st Lace Panel.

INSTRUCTIONS FOR THE SWEATER

5-Stitch Lace Panel

Rnds 1, 3, and 5 Yo, ssk, k1, k2tog, yo.

Rnd 2 and all even rnds K5.

Rnd 7 K5.

Rnds 9, 11 and 13 K2tog, yo, k1, yo, ssk.

Rnds 15 and 16 K5.

Rep Rnds 1–16 for 5LP.

Neck

With shorter needle, CO 72 sts. Join, taking care

not to twist sts on needle. Pm to indicate beg of rnd and sl marker every rnd. Cont as folls: *p1, work Rnd 1 of 5LP; rep from * around. Cont 5LP as established, working p1, 5LP for 23 more rnds.

Yoke

Next (inc) rnd *P1, work 5LP, M1 p-wise; rep from * around—84 sts.

Next 3 rnds *P1, 5LP, p1; rep from * around.

First set of lace panel insertions

Change to longer needle when needed.

Next (inc) rnd *P1, 5LP, p1, yo; rep from * around 11 times more—96 sts.

Next rnd *P1, 5LP, p1, k1; rep from * around.

Next (inc) rnd *P1, 5LP, p1, yo, k1, yo; rep from * around—120 sts.

Next rnd *P1, 5LP, p1, k3; rep from * around.

Next (inc) rnd *P1, 5LP, p1, yo, k3, yo; rep from * around—144 sts.

Next rnd *P1, 5LP, p1, k5; rep from * around.

Next 12 (16, 10, 10) rnds *P1, 5LP; rep from * around.

Second set of lace panel insertions

Next (inc) rnd *P1, 5LP, M1 p-wise; rep from * around 23 times more—168 sts.

5-ST LACE PANEL

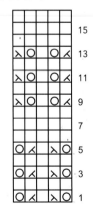

15
13
11
9
7
5
3
1

KEY

☐ K ON RS

⊠ YARN OVER (YO)

⊠ SSK ON RS

⊠ K2TOG ON RS

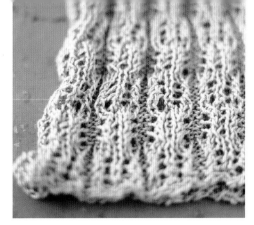

Next rnd *[P1, 5LP, p1] 3 (2, 2, 2) times, yo; rep from * 7 (11, 11, 11) times more.
Next rnd *[P1, 5LP, p1] 3 (2, 2, 2) times, k1; rep from * around.
Next rnd *[P1, 5LP, p1] 3 (2, 2, 2) times, yo, k1, yo; rep from * around.
Next rnd *[P1, 5LP, p1] 3 (2, 2, 2) times, k3; rep from * around.
Next rnd *[P1,5LP, p1] 3 (2, 2, 2) times, yo, k3, yo; rep from * around.
Next rnd *[P1, 5LP, p1] 3 (2, 2, 2) times, k5; rep from * around.
Next (inc) rnd *[P1, 5LP, p1] 3 (2, 2, 2) times, M1 p-wise, 5LP, M1 p-wise; rep from * around—224 (252, 252, 252) sts.
Next 25 (30, 10, 10) rnds *P1, 5LP, p1; rep from * 31 (35, 35, 35) times more.

For sizes Small and Medium Only

Proceed to divide for body and sleeves.

For size Large only

Third set of lace panel inserts

Next rnd *[P1, 5LP, p1] 9 times, yo; rep from * 3 times more.
Next rnd *[P1, 5LP, p1] 9 times, k1; rep from * around.
Next rnd * [P1, 5LP, p1] 9 times, yo, k1, yo; rep from * around.
Next rnd * [P1, 5LP, p1] 9 times, k3; rep from * around.
Next rnd * [P1, 5LP, p1] 9 times, yo, k3, yo; rep from * around.
Next rnd * [P1, 5LP, p1] 9 times, k5; rep from * around.
Next (inc) rnd * [P1, 5LP, p1] 9 times, M1 p-wise, 5LP, M1 p-wise; rep from * around—280 sts.
Next 30 rnds *P1, 5LP, p1; rep from * 39 times more. Proceed to divide for body and sleeves.

For size X-Large only

Third set of lace panel inserts

Next rnd * [P1, 5LP, p1] 5 times, yo, [P1, 5LP, p1] 4 times, yo; rep from * 3 times more.
Next rnd * [P1, 5LP, p1] 5 times, k1, [P1, 5LP, p1] 4 times, k1; rep from * around.

Next rnd * [P1, 5LP, p1] 5 times, yo, k1, yo, [P1, 5LP, p1] 4 times, yo, k1, yo; rep from * around.
Next rnd * [P1, 5LP, p1] 5 times, k3, [P1, 5LP, p1] 4 times, k3; rep from * around.
Next rnd * [P1, 5LP, p1] 5 times, yo, k3, yo, [P1, 5LP, p1] 4 times, yo, k3, yo; rep from * around.
Next rnd * [P1, 5LP, p1] 5 times, k5, [P1, 5LP, p1] 4 times, k5; rep from * around.
Next (inc) rnd * [P1, 5LP, p1] 5 times, M1 p-wise, 5LP, M1 p-wise, [P1, 5LP, p1] 4 times, M1 p-wise, 5LP, M1 p-wise; rep from * around—308 sts.
Next 30 rnds *P1, 5LP, p1; rep from * 43 times more. Proceed to divide for body and sleeves.

Divide for body and sleeves

Using waste yarn, CO 2 sets of 14 sts and leave on a spare needle.
Next rnd *[P1, 5LP, p1] 10 (11, 12, 13) times; work across 14 sts from spare needle as folls: [p1, k5, p1] twice; place next 42 (49, 56, 63) sts on a holder for sleeve; rep from * once more—168 (182, 196, 210) sts for body.

Body

Join and pm to indicate beg of rnd. Work even in (p1, 5LP, p1) until body measures 14¾"/37.5cm or desired length to underarm, end with Rnd 6 or 14. BO all sts *very loosely* in pat st.

Sleeves

Slip sts from holder to larger, 16" needle. Undo waste yarn of CO edge of underarms and place 14 sts on spare needles. Join yarn, beg at middle of underarm, work 7 underarm sts, work across 42 (49, 56, 63) sts in pat as established, work 7 underarm sts—56 (63, 70, 77) sts. Join and pm to indicate beg of rnd. Work 15 rnds even. Dec 1 st at each side of marker, with 2 sts between decs, on next, then every 16th rnd 6 times more—42 (49, 56, 63) sts. Work even until sleeve measures 18"/45.5cm or desired length, end with rnd 6 or 14. BO all sts *very loosely* in pat st.

FINISHING

With a tapestry needle, weave in loose yarn tails to the WS of work and secure. Block same as for swatch.

LOUET

LOUET SELLS LINEN, MERINO, MERLIN (MERINO LINEN), ROVING, SPINNING WHEELS, AND OTHER EQUIPMENT.

The colors of Louet's linen yarns are lovely, and owner Trudy Van Stralen says that because she knows Mother Nature does it best, she first dyes yarn with natural colors and then uses commercial colors to mimic the natural original. Trudy is the author of a book on plant-dying titled *Indigo, Madder and Marigold: A Portfolio of Colors from Natural Dyes*. By duplicating the color of natural dyes with commercial colors, she achieves beautiful results and she doesn't have to worry about finding the actual dyestuffs every time she wants to dye yarn.

Opposite
A coarse fiber, spun hemp is shown here.

THE OTHER BAST FIBERS

In addition to linen, the other fibers in the bast family include hemp, ramie, and jute. Grown and cultivated for centuries throughout the world, the bast fibers are noted for their exceptional strength, and have traditionally been used in the manufacture of cording and rope making; knitting is just a short step away.

"Bast" fibers are the long, strong fibers that create the outer layer of the plant stalk. The process of harvesting the bast from hemp begins with separating the fibers from the stalks. This is the retting process, in which the stalks are left to lie in the fields to rot; soaking them in water can accelerate the process. When the stalks are softened, they are washed to remove the outer surface and then pounded to separate the useful outer layers (the bast) from the interior of the stalk. The bast is then combed to prepare it for spinning.

Hemp

The Natural Knitter would not be complete without granting special attention to the cultivation of hemp and its appeal to the environmentally conscious. Requiring virtually no pesticides or herbicides to grow successfully, hemp is naturally resistant to bacteria, mold, and pests. As a crop, it can be grown year after year in the same soil and is also a profitable rotation crop for those practicing sustainable agriculture.

Mired in political controversy (as of this writing, growing fiber-producing hemp in the United States is illegal) hemp is a member of the same plant family as marijuana, *Cannabis sativa*. Contrary to common belief, there are two distinct species, defined by the levels of psychoactive ingredient tetrahydrocannabinol, or THC for short, contained in the plant. Industrial hemp, which is grown for the stems required to make fiber, contains less than 1 percent THC. Recreational hemp (marijuana), on the other hand, contains 3–20 percent THC. Hemp fiber, fabric, and clothing currently available in the United States are primarily manufactured in hemp-producing countries, including Canada and China.

"Male" hemp plants are harvested early and produce a fine fiber that is suitable for the production of yarn. The "female" hemp plants are harvested later in the season and produce a heavier fiber that is used for rope making and canvas.

The use of hemp for rope making dates back thousands of years to its cultivation in China as early as 2800 BC. Centuries later it was a key crop in the colonial Americas (when not serving as president, both Thomas Jefferson and George Washington were hemp farmers) and used for ship sails, ropes, and linens. Hemp's popularity declined in the 1800s when cotton became the fiber of choice for clothing production.

Knitting with hemp is best done on bamboo or wooden needles, as it will help to keep from dropping stitches. And unlike wool, it has little or no give, but drapes beautifully and takes dye easily. Hemp lends itself well to knitting mesh bags, airy overtops, or just about anything that one would use cotton for.

Cast-Off Sweater

DESIGNED BY DEBBIE NEW

The unusual netlike stitch used in this garment looks as if it couldn't possibly be knitted. It grew out of experiments with creating a loose bind-off (cast-off). The pattern row is worked by passing the previous stitch over the one just knitted. But every stitch is double wrapped and only one of the wraps is lifted over, leaving the other wrap still in place on the needle. So when the row is finished, half of each wrapped stitch is still on the needle and the number of stitches remains unchanged. The resulting fabric has lines of twisted stitches separated by a single horizontal line. Knitted loosely, it looks like open drapey netting. Knitted more tightly, it looks woven.

The net look of this stitch worked in hemp reflects the traditional uses for this sturdy fiber, once a staple for string and rope, but now being used for comfortable knitted garments that soften and drape with wear. Although the hemp yarn can shrink up to 10 percent with washing, this does not seem to alter the size of the garment as washing also makes the stitches less crisp and flattens and evens them.

Skill Level
Experienced

Sizes
This is a knit-to-your-own-size garment. Size shown is for 36"/91.5cm bust.

Finished Measurements (of sweaters shown)
Short-sleeve sweater Bust 40"/102cm
Long-sleeve sweater Bust 36"/91.5cm
Short-sleeve length (center to cuff) 15"/38cm
Long-sleeve length (center to cuff) 26"/66cm
Both versions Length 19"/48cm
Neck width 7¼"/18.5cm

Yarn
Short-sleeve sweater
EXPRESSIONS 2-PLY by House of Hemp (UK), 1¾oz/50g skeins, each approx 186yd/170m (100% hemp) or a fine weight yarn
• 3 skeins in HaHa
Long-sleeve sweater
ALLHEMP3 by Lana Knits (Can), 1½oz/45g skeins, each approx 145yd/132m (100% hemp) or a fine weight yarn
• 4 skeins in Avocado

Needles & Notions
• Sizes 7 and 10½ (4.5mm and 6.5mm) circular needles or size needed to obtain gauge
• Eight small ring stitch markers or yarn markers
• Two stitch holders or waste yarn
• Tapestry needle

Gauge
16 sts and 25 rnds = 4"/10 cm in St st using larger circular needle.
Adjust the needle size if necessary to obtain the correct gauge.

Gauges
Short-sleeve sweater
17 sts and 12 rows = 4"/10cm over cast-off st using larger needles.
Long-sleeve sweater
17 sts and 14 rows = 4"/10cm over cast-off st using larger needles or your swatch gauge.
Adjust the needle size if necessary to obtain the correct gauge.

Construction Notes

1) These sweaters are worked from the top down and have an octagonal shape.

2) The garter stitch neck edging is worked back and forth, after which the yoke is worked in "cast off" stitch in the round.

3) When the yoke is the desired width, the sleeve "octagon sections" are put on hold to be worked later and the body is knit to the desired length and finished with a garter edge.

4) The sleeves are worked last. The short-sleeve version finishes immediately with a garter edging and the long sleeves are worked with or without shaping, according to the knitter's taste.

GLOSSARY

⬚ **kfb** Inc by knitting into front then back of st.

⬚ **pfb** Inc by purling into front then back of st.

⬚ **dw** Work a k st by double wrapping (i.e., wrapping yarn twice around needle before pulling st through).

⬚ **pwso** Pass a single wrap from the previous st over the st just knitted.

⬚ **3-needle bindoff** Holding needles parallel with RS together and WS facing, k2tog from front and back needles, *k2tog from front and back needles and pass the first st over the second to bind off; rep from * to end.

SWATCH WORKSHOP

The garment pattern is not difficult, but the stitch pattern is unusual, so it is a good idea to try a sample of the stitch before beginning the yoke. The swatch serves as a mini-workshop. Use this swatch to learn how to work the stitch evenly and to quickly correct any mistakes that might crop up. Note that the stitch will look somewhat uneven before washing because of the springy nature of the yarn.

Begin the Swatch

With smaller needle, CO 20 sts using the cable method. Work 5 rows in garter st. Change to larger needle.

Double wrap (dw) row (RS) Insert tip of RH needle into first stitch on LH needle, then wrap the yarn twice around the right needle tip before pulling the stitch (2 wraps) through. (**Note:** If you normally hold the yarn in your *left* hand, do this by picking the thread with the right needle as if to work a knit stitch, then picking it again in the same direction so that it wraps around twice. If you normally hold the yarn in your *right* hand, wrap the yarn around the needle tip as if to work a knit stitch, then wrap it again in the same direction to make the double wrap. Then, for either method, pull both wraps through the stitch on the LH needle to complete the stitch. Your first stitch should now have two wraps coming up through the stitch below it.)

Work a second dw stitch and pass a single wrap from the first pair over both wraps of the second (pwso). You will find that one of the wraps of the first stitch (the correct one) is easy to lift and the other is not. You will now have a single wrap from the first stitch on the RH needle and both wraps of the second stitch.

Work a third dw and pwso. You should now have two single wraps and a double wrap on the RH needle. Work dw, pwso to the end of the row, then pass one wrap of the last stitch over the other, so that it, too, finishes with a single wrap on the needle.

NELSON, BRITISH COLUMBIA–BASED LANAKNITS DESIGNS, IS A MAIL-ORDER MANUFACTURER

of hemp and hemp-blend yarns. The business's owner, Lana Hames, took her passion for knitting to the next level when she opened "shop" in 2000 after three years of planning.

Inspired by a trip to the industry trade show Stitches East, she seized the opportunity to capitalize on hemp, which is widely grown throughout Canada. In addition to

hemp yarns, Lana also offers patterns that enhance the unique characteristics inherent in hemp (see page 136). Lana's mantra for her eco-friendly yarn? "Hemp, Hemp, Hooray!"

Purl row (WS) P2tog, purl to last stitch then inc by purling into the front then the back of the stitch (pfb). Work these two rows for the cast-off pat st. (**Note:** *These rows are for working the stitch back and forth only. When knitting in the round, the "purl row" is knit.*)

Hints for Double Wrap Row (RS)

1) When passing the previous wrap over, be careful to lift the wrap only; don't also pick up the single wrap of the stitch before it.

2) Try not to stretch the wrap as you lift it over. Push the right needle well in when knitting the wrapped stitch, but keep stitches near the right needle tip when lifting the wrap over.

3) If one wrap slips off the last stitch, replace it by pulling the back of the stitch back with the left needle and wrapping the right needle (purlwise) again.

4) When unpicking a few stitches, the last stitch will have a single twisted wrap on it. Find the wrap that has been passed over the stitch and replace it on the right needle tip.

5) Watch the horizontal line you are making as you work. If there is a break in it, go back and fix it because you won't be able to fix it in a later row.

Hint for Purl Row (WS)

Make sure that each stitch on left needle is twisted with the top thread angling up to the left before you knit into it.

Finish the swatch

Work about 6"/15cm, then change to the smaller needle, work a few rows of garter st, then BO all sts loosely. Wash the swatch and lay flat to dry. Measure your gauge from this swatch.

INSTRUCTIONS FOR THE SWEATER

Yoke

With smaller needle and using a cable cast-on, [CO 12 sts, pm] 8 times—96 sts. Work back and forth in garter st as folls:

Row 1 Knit.

Row 2 [Kfb, k10, kfb, slip marker] 8 times—112 sts. Knit next 3 rows. Change to larger needle. Join, taking care not to twist sts on needle. Pm to indicate beg of rnd and sl marker every rnd.

Rnd 1 [(Kfb) twice, knit to marker (check for mistakes)] 7 times, [kfb] twice, knit to 1 st before marker, dw last stitch—128 sts.

Rnd 2 Dw first st, pass the wrap from the previous st over both the marker and the new st, dw the next st and take the previous wrap over the new st, but not the marker (as this would trap the marker). *Dw, pwso; rep from * to last st of rnd, k1, pwso. Rep Rnds 1 and 2 until two sections are wide enough for half the body width (see Note) when the octagon is laid out with the miter lying as in the diagram, on next passes end with Rnd 1. (**Note:** At this point one section should be 1.1 times half the desired finished body width, that is, half the body width plus 1/10. So for a finished body width of 20"/51cm, the work should measure 11"/27.5 cm between each marker. There is no need to add ease to a garment to be worn over a tank top or swimsuit, so use 1.1 x ¼ the actual bust measurement to determine body width. But for a looser garment, first add 2"/5cm, or the desired amount of ease, to the bust measurement.

Body

Rnd 1 *Dw, pwso; rep from * for two body sections. Slip the sts of the next two sections onto a holding thread for a sleeve. *Dw, pwso; rep for two sections, but single wrap the last st as before. Slip the stitches of the next two sections onto a holding thread. Make sure there are still markers between all 4 sections.

Rnd 2 *Knit to center, sm, [kfb] twice, knit to 4 sts before underarm marker, [k2tog] twice, sm; rep from * once for the remaining 2 body sections, but dw the last k2tog st of the round. (**Note:** You are working the first and third sections without increases or decreases. The double side decreases compensate for the continuing double increases at the center so that the side seams are straight.)

Rnd 3 *Dw, pwso; rep from * to last st of rnd, k1, pwso. Rep Rnds 2 and 3 until body is desired length. (**Note:** If you wish, after a few rounds, you can slip half the body stitches onto the smaller needle or waste yarn so you can try the garment on to see whether you like the fit of the body width you have chosen.) For body length, work until the underarm decrease miter reaches waist length, or a bit longer, as desired.

End with Rnd 2 without double wrapping the last

stitch. Change to smaller needle. Working back and forth, and starting with a WS row, work 3 rows of garter stitch.

Next row K2tog at the beg and end of the row and on either side of the underarm marker, and work a kfb on either side of markers at the center front and back. Knit next 2 rows. Change to larger needle and BO all sts. Seam the small selvedge edge of the garter border.

Sleeves

Starting at the underarm, slip the stitches of the first sleeve onto larger needle, with the marker still in place at the center. If your needle is too long to bring the end stitches to the needle tips, draw a loop of the flexible shank out between the center stitches, or use a shorter needle. There will be a gap between the two ends of the round. To close this gap, use a spare needle to pick up and knit a stitch into two or 3 strands below the gap. Then, continuing to use the spare needle, work a 3-needle bindoff until you have bound off 6 sts from each needle tip. Place the last stitch on the right needle and pass a stitch over it.

Short sleeves
Complete garter border as for the body.

Long sleeves
The sleeve can be worked exactly the same way as the body. For those who don't like working small circles, work back and forth as folls:

Row 1 (RS) Dw, *pwso, dw; rep from * to end, pass the last dw over itself.

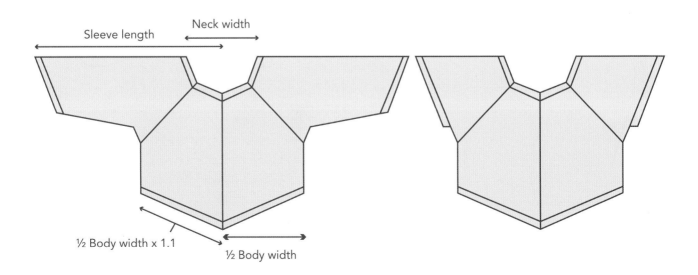

Sleeve length

Neck width

½ Body width x 1.1

½ Body width

HABU TEXTILES

TAKAKO UEKI ESTABLISHED HABU TEXTILES IN 1999 AS A STUDIO FOR HANDWOVEN TEXTILES CREATED by herself and by Japanese and American handweavers. A year later, she opened a New York showroom to introduce simple but unusual textiles and yarns to the American public. Takako believes that "yarn is the soul of fabric. Without ones made with good care, the fabrics will not live long."

Habu's textiles are distinguished by the unusual yarns used to construct them; these are imported from Japan and rarely available in the United States. Takako has made many trips to Japan over the years, searching out these unique yarns and cultivating relationships with their suppliers.

Habu's portfolio includes more than 450 yarn selections, including silk and stainless steel, pine paper, pineapple, bamboo, hand-tie ramies, cashmere with almost no twist, naturally gold silks, handspun silks/cottons, silk stainless steel, and even fine silver.

Row 2 [P2tog] twice, purl to 2 sts before marker, [pfb] twice, sm, purl to end. Rep these 2 rows until sleeve is desired length.

Tapering the sleeve

The sleeves have no shaping, but can be tapered by working the alternate dec row instead of Row 2 every 6th row as folls:

Alternate dec row [P2tog] 3 times, purl to 2 sts before marker, [pfb] twice, knit to 2 sts before end, p2tog. Complete garter border as for body, inc on either side of the center marker, and dec at the edges every 4th row.

FINISHING

Long sleeves

Seam the bottom of the sleeve by lining up the horizontal lines and stitching twice through each pair.

Both versions

Wash and block sweater as you did for your swatch.

Ramie

In use for more than 6,000 years, ramie (also known as grass cloth or China linen) is one of the oldest plant fibers cultivated specifically for fabric production. Produced primarily in China and other Asian countries, the naturally white, fine, lustrous material from the plant was used in Chinese burial shrouds more than 2,000 years ago, predating cotton in Asia.

Ramie fibers are obtained from the stem of the Asian perennial shrub that is known scientifically as *Bohemeria nivea*. The crop can sustain harvesting up to six times a year. Purists might not classify ramie as "natural" because, unlike the other bast plants, ramie requires chemical processing to de-gum the fiber.

Although rigid in nature and often mistaken for linen, ramie is more porous, which makes it more absorbent than other cellulose fibers, such as cotton and linen. It is also one of the strongest natural fibers; when wet, it is even stronger, and does not shrink or lose its shape. It dries quickly and with repeated washings grows more lustrous. Today, not only does ramie's unique texture lend itself to creating sturdy knits, it also is used in such common products as straw hats, fish netting, upholstery, and wallpaper.

Pineapple Overtop

DESIGNED BY SETSUKO TORII

Who would think that the leaves of the pineapple plant would produce a strong, white, silky fiber? Setsuko Torii saw the possibilities when designing this wonderfully lacy overtop using the crisp pineapple yarn from Habu Textiles.

Skill Level
Easy

Size
Instructions are for one size fits most. See Designer Note for making garment smaller or larger.

Finished Measurements
Bust 44½"/113cm
Length 26"/66cm

Yarn
YARN #XS-37 by Habu Textiles, 1oz/28g skeins, each approx 780yds/713m (100% pineapple fiber) or a super fine weight yarn

• 5 skeins in #1 Natural

Needles & Notions
• One pair size 8 (5mm) needles *or size needed to obtain gauge*

• Tapestry needle

Gauge
18 sts and 30 rows = 4"/10cm over pat st with 3 strands held tog and size 8 (5mm) needles (after blocking).

Adjust the needle size as necessary to obtain the gauge desired.

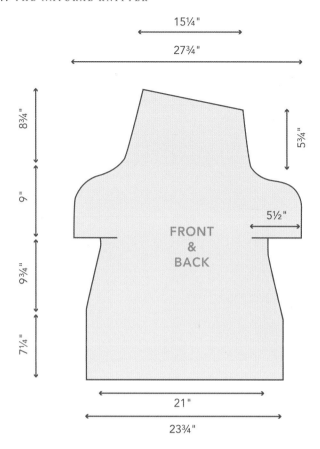

15¼"

27¾"

8¾"

5¾"

9"

9¾"

5½"

FRONT
&
BACK

7¼"

21"

23¾"

Note

Work with 3 strands of yarn held tog throughout.

Designer Note

Work at a somewhat tighter or looser gauge, or change needle size, to make a smaller or larger garment.

Construction Notes

1) The garment pieces (front and back) are worked at a very loose gauge back and forth from the bottom up.
2) Work decreases in pattern as established.
3) The collar is asymmetrical and requires special shaping; the decreases and bindoffs are worked at different rates on each side.
4) Follow instructions closely for each side of the fabric, but if you get a bit off on your count, it is not critical.

GLOSSARY

✄ **Dec row** K1 (selvedge st), k2tog (or p2tog), work in pat as established to last 3 sts, k2 tog (or p2tog), k1 (selvedge st).

✄ **Block Stitch Pattern**
(multiple of 10 sts plus 7)
Rows 1, 3, and 5 (RS) K1 (selvedge st), *k5, p5; rep from *, end k5, k1 (selvedge st).

Rows 2, 4, and 6 K1 (selvedge st), *p5, k5; rep from *, end p5, k1 (selvedge st).
Rows 7, 9, and 11 Rep Row 2.
Rows 8, 10, and 12 Rep Row 1.
Rep Rows 1–12 for block st pat.

INSTRUCTIONS FOR THE TOP

Back

Using 3 strands of yarn held tog, *loosely* CO 107 sts. Work even in Block St pat for 7¼"/18.5cm, end with a WS row. Maintaining selvedge sts, work Dec row on next, then every 10th row 5 times more—95 sts. Work even until piece measures 17"/43cm from beg, end with row 12.

Armhole shaping
BO 10 sts at beg of next 2 rows, then CO 25 sts at beg of foll 2 rows—125 sts. Work even in pat as established for 1½"/4cm.

Shoulder shaping
Work Dec row on next row, then every 6th row 3 times more, every 4th row 3 times, every other row 5 times, *every* row 4 times, every other row 3 times, then every row 6 times. BO 3 sts at the beg of next 2 rows—69 sts.

Collar shaping
Please read through this entire section before beg to work, and refer to chart.
At the beg of row, BO 2 sts once, then dec 1 st every other row 3 times, every 4th row twice, then every 6th row 3 times. Work 8 rows even, then BO 4 sts at beg of row 10 times, then 3 sts twice—total of 46 sts BO at beg of rows. AT THE SAME TIME, *at the end of row,* dec 1 st every other row 5 times, every 4th row 4 times, every 6th row twice, every 8th row twice, then work even until final BO at beg of row is completed—total of 13 sts dec at end of rows. You should have no more sts when you have completed all beg of row BOs. However, if you do, simply bind them off.

Front

Work as for back.

FINISHING

Block pieces to measurements. Sew side, shoulder and collar seams. Gather the sleeve cap to 8"/20cm and sew CO edges to underarm BO's to form armhole. With a tapestry needle, weave in loose yarn tails to the WS of work and secure.

Pineapple

In certain climates, such as in the Philippines, the pineapple plant is cultivated specifically for fiber production. When the pineapples are young, they are removed from the plant to direct growth to the leaves. The leaves are scraped to remove the pulp, and the fibers are then rinsed, dried, and combed to prepare them for spinning. Although pineapple is not readily available outside the Philippines, Habu textiles offers it in the United States. Similar in appearance to linen, it is lightweight, and it's usually blended with other fibers, such as silk, giving it an elegant appearance. Care is easy, as pineapple is sturdy and washable.

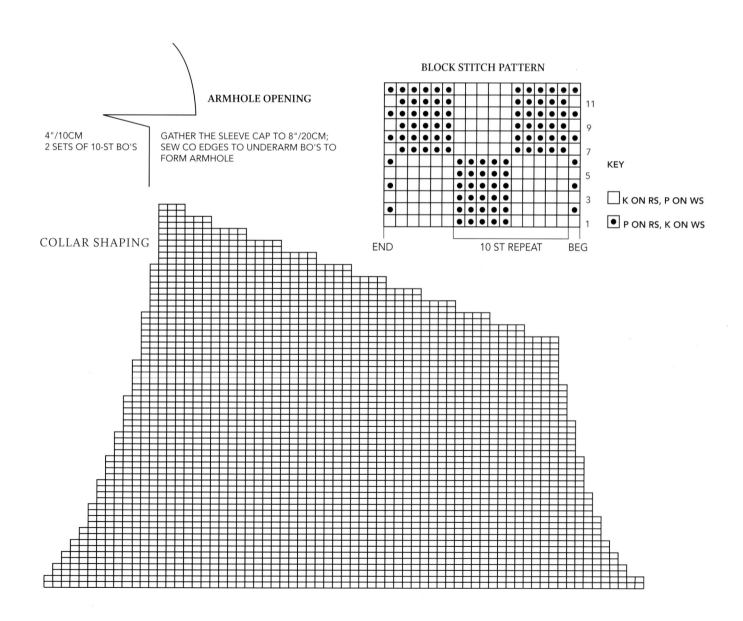

ARMHOLE OPENING

4"/10CM
2 SETS OF 10-ST BO'S

GATHER THE SLEEVE CAP TO 8"/20CM;
SEW CO EDGES TO UNDERARM BO'S TO
FORM ARMHOLE

BLOCK STITCH PATTERN

KEY

☐ K ON RS, P ON WS

▣ P ON RS, K ON WS

END   10 ST REPEAT   BEG

COLLAR SHAPING

Chapter 4
PLANT-DYED FIBERS

Serendipitously people around the world were figuring out how to dye fibers. Since prehistoric times (13,000 BC), people have been coloring with plant dyes, which offer a much richer sensory experience than textiles dyed with the synthetic dyes mostly used today.

For instance, contrast the gaudiness of fluorescent yellow and orange synthetic dyes with the rich, subtle hues from dyeing with goldenrod flowers and madder root. Dyeing yarns and fleeces with dyes you create from plants, barks, roots, and foods is a never-ending source of wonderful colors and a great activity to do by yourself or with a group! The next time you are on a hike or in your garden, take a look around to see if there is something you can use as a dye. While goldenrod is mainly perceived as a weed, it is a *wonderful* source of beautiful golden yellow.

Depending on where you get your dyestuffs, there are different plants available, some better than others. For instance, most people would imagine that beets would be a great dye because of their rich color. Unfortunately, beets will be a disappointment.

Whether you are dyeing fiber, yarn, or a finished product, make sure to keep precise records every time. If you achieve a color that you love, this will help in re-creating it. Conversely, if a color that is not to your taste, you will never have to venture there again.

Silk, wool, mohair, and other animal fibers accept dye well, whereas cotton, linen, and other plant fibers require a more extensive mordant process to be successful (see "Mordants Matter" sidebar, p. 150). To achieve the most even coloring, use a fiber that has been washed to remove oils, which will cloud and mottle the final color.

There are many variables that can affect the dye process. Do you live in an arid or humid climate? Season, altitude, the minerals in the dye water, even the odor of the plant dye—all can affect the final product. Fresh plants produce the most intense dyes, while dried plants yield a more muted hue.

It is important to note that some dyestuffs can be poisonous. Consult the local cooperative extension service to see what poisonous plants are indigenous to your region. (None of the plant dyes shown here are poisonous. See the Resources section for purveyors of dyestuff.)

An easy and precise recipe for making onion skin dye follows on the next page, but simply use it as a jumping-off point!

One of the easiest ways to get started along the natural dye path is with **onion skins.** They are readily available and create a warm, golden color.

Right
Each mordant affects the dye differently and will create varied colors. From middle top clockwise, the five mordants are: copper, alum, iron, tin, and chrome.

Opposite
The following plants all make excellent natural dyes, clockwise from upper left, eucalyptus, mullen, black walnuts, dried marigolds, oak galls, and mallow.

Easy Onion Skin Dye Project

You Will Need

- 8 ounces of yarn or fleece
- 2 tablespoons alum
- 8 ounces of onion skins
- Cheesecloth and string to tie it closed or nylon hosiery leg
- Large pot (enameled lobster pots work well)

INSTRUCTIONS

1) Soak the fiber in water, just enough to cover the yarn, so it is thoroughly wet.

2) Dissolve the alum in the same pot.

3) Heat the water just to simmering. Simmer for about 1 hour.

4) Meanwhile, place the onion skins in the cheesecloth or hosiery and tie to secure all the skins inside. (If the skins escape, you will end up picking out pieces of onion skins from the dyed yarn or fiber later.) Place this package in the dye pot along with the wet yarn or fiber and return it to a simmer.

5) Simmer, stirring occasionally, until the yarn is a color you are happy with. (Surprisingly, onion skins deliver a golden color whether they are yellow- or red-skinned onions. I had to check this out for myself and it was true!)

6) Check the yarn to make sure the whole batch is the color you want, then remove the yarn and rinse it thoroughly. Dry and knit on.

Mordants Matter!

Before you dye fiber, you can "mordant" the fiber, or soak it in a water bath that includes a mordant, which can be a naturally occurring metal salt that acts as a fixative. A mordant—the word means "to bite" in Latin—opens up fibers, allowing them to absorb the dye better. Most dyestuffs need a mordant, and, depending on which one you use, the results can vary a lot or a little, as the mordant changes the fiber chemically. The most common mordants are:

ALUM (potassium aluminum sulfate)

CHROME (potassium dichromate)

TIN (stannous chloride)

COPPER (copper sulfate)

IRON (ferrous sulfate)

Mordants can be toxic—alum the least—and there is much dispute as to the toxicity of chrome. Always dye in a well-ventilated space, preferably outdoors. It is best practice to use gloves, goggles, a mask, and an apron when dyeing.

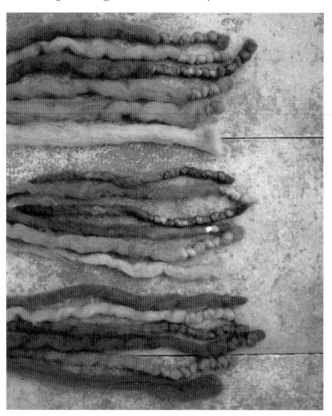

Each cluster of yarn has been treated with a different plant dye: madder, logwood, and cocineal (from top to bottom). However, the knotted strands in each cluster have been treated with a different mordant (strands without a knot have no mordant). Alum was used in strands that have one knot, chrome in strands with two knots, tin in strands with three knots, copper in strands with four knots, and iron in strands with five knots.

Step 1: Weighing the onion skins.

Step 2: Onion skins placed into cheesecloth before being submerged in the dye bath (step 4 at left).

Step 3: Stirring the yarn as it is being dyed (step 5 at left).

Step 4: Checking the yarn as it is being dyed (step 6 at left).

It's a Mod, Mod, Modular Hat, Socks, and Half-Gloves

DESIGNED BY DARLENE HAYES

The design concept for these pieces grew out of Darlene Hayes's fascination with the ripples that form on still water when a pebble is tossed into it—all those peaks and valleys spreading out from the center point. The designer worked up one version in several different blues, but all the other wonderful colors that she had at her disposal were clamoring to be included. As a result, what started out as a study of water turned into something more akin to a pop art project.

Skill Levels

Hat Intermediate

Gloves and Socks
Experienced

Size

Instructions are for women's size Medium. See Designer Note for making hat, gloves and socks smaller or larger.

Finished Measurements

Hat
Head circumference
22½"/57cm

Gloves
Hand circumference
6¾"/17cm

Socks
Foot circumference
7½"/19cm

Yarn

FINGERING WEIGHT YARN by Nature's Palette, 1¾oz/50g skeins, each approx 185yd/169m (100% merino wool) or a super fine weight yarn

Hat
• 1 skein in NP-104 Medium Indigo (A)

Gloves
• 1 skein in NP-104 Medium Indigo (A)

Socks
• 2 skeins in NP-104 Medium Indigo (A)

For all projects
• 1 skein each in NP-124 Orchid (B), NP-134 Coral Bells (C), NP-122 Spring Grass (D) and NP-108 Accacia (E)

Needles & Notions

Hat
• One set (5) size 4 (3.5mm) double-pointed needles (dpns) *or size needed to obtain gauge*

• Two size 4 (3.5mm) circular needles, 16"/40cm long *or size needed to obtain gauge*

Gloves
• One set (5) size 3 (3.25mm) double-pointed needles (dpns) *or size needed to obtain gauge*

Socks
• One set (5) each sizes 1 and 2 (2.25mm and 2.75mm) double-pointed needles (dpns) *or size needed to obtain gauge*

For all projects
• Size H/8 (5mm) or larger crochet hook

• Tapestry needle

• Smooth sport-weight waste yarn

Gauges

Hat
26 sts and 36 rnds = 4"/10cm over St st using larger needles (3.5mm).

Gloves
28 sts and 40 rnds = 4"/10cm over St st using smaller (3.25mm) dpns.

Socks
32 sts and 44 rnds = 4"/10cm over St st using larger dpns.

Adjust the needle sizes as necessary to obtain correct gauges.

Designer Note

Work at a somewhat tighter or looser gauge, or change needle sizes, to make hat, gloves, or socks smaller or larger.

Construction Notes

1) Each of the pieces in this ensemble starts with an "anchor piece" from which squares are worked.
2) These squares are based on a very simple modular-square system; each is started with a provisional cast-on and worked from the outside edge in.
3) The provisional cast-on is removed, then some of those live stitches are used as part of the start for the next square. It may sound complicated, and it takes a lot of words to explain, but once you get the basic concept it is pretty smooth sailing.

GLOSSARY

❊ **S2KP2** Slip 2 tog as if to knit, k1, pass slipped sts over. This is a centered double decrease.
❊ **N1, N2, N3, N4** Needle 1, Needle 2, Needle 3, Needle 4.
❊ **Provisional cast-on** Using a size H/8 (5mm) or larger crochet hook and waste yarn, crochet a single chain 5 or 10 sts longer than your total number of cast-on stitches; fasten off. Using project needle and yarn, knit up 1 st in each of the "purl-like" bumps on the back of the chain for as many cast-on sts indicated in the pattern. To remove waste yarn, undo the last crochet chain and pull; the chain will "unzip." As you pull, put live sts on waste yarn or needle as instructed.

BASIC SQUARE

First row starting square

Slip 15 sts from your "anchor piece" (see individual pats) onto a dpn. Using waste yarn and B, provisionally cast on 45 more sts—60 sts total. Divide these sts evenly onto 3 more dpns (15 sts each needle). Cont to work as folls:

Rnd 1 With B, k58.
Rnd 2 With A, [S2KP2, k12] 4 times—52 sts.
Rnd 3 With A, p50.
Rnd 4 With C, [S2KP2, k10] 4 times—44 sts.
Rnd 5 With C, k42.
Rnd 6 With A, [S2KP2, k8] 4 times—36 sts.
Rnd 7 With A, p34.
Rnd 8 With A, [S2KP2, k6] 4 times—28 sts.
Rnd 9 With A, p26.
Rnd 10 With D, [S2KP2, k4] 4 times—20 sts.
Rnd 11 With D, k18.
Rnd 12 With A, [S2KP2, k2] 4 times—12 sts.
Rnd 13 With A, p10.
Rnd 14 With E, [S2KP2] 4 times—4 sts. Cut yarn and using tapestry needle, thread tail through last 4 sts. Remove the yarn used for the cast-on and put the live sts on a piece of waste yarn until needed.

First row middle square

Slip 15 sts from the left (as it is facing you) cast-on edge of the square last worked to a needle. Slip 15 sts from the "anchor piece" to a second needle. Using waste yarn and B, provisionally cast on 30 more sts—60 sts total. Work as for First Row starting square.

First row end square

Slip 15 sts from the left (as it is facing you) cast-on edge of the square last worked to a needle. Slip 15 sts from the "anchor piece" to a second needle. Slip 15 sts from the right edge of the first row starting square to a third needle. Using waste yarn and B, provisionally cast on 15 more sts—60 sts total. Work as for first row starting square.

Second row starting square

Slip 15 sts from the top of a first row square onto a needle (see Note below). Using waste yarn and B, provisionally cast on 45 more sts—60 sts total. Divide these sts evenly onto 3 more dpns (15 sts each needle). Work as for first row starting square.

Second row middle square

Set up and work as for first row middle square using sts from the top of a first row square in place of sts from the "anchor piece."

Second row end square

Set up and work as for first row end square using sts from the top of a first row square in place of sts from the "anchor piece."

Note

You may find when working with second row squares that you can only find 14 stitches from the provisional cast-on edge instead of the required 15. Do not despair. This is a result of the change in the direction of knitting. You will conveniently have a loose tail of yarn at the appropriate spot, so thread it onto a tapestry needle, loop it over your knitting needle to make a stitch and secure it in the knitted fabric. You may also notice small holes visible at the point where the corners of the individual squares meet (another result of changing the direction of the knitting). Again, use one of those convenient yarn ends to sew the hole closed.

INSTRUCTIONS FOR THE HAT

Anchor piece

Using circular needle and A, CO 135 sts. Work in St st for 1"/2.5cm. Using second circular needle, pick up and knit 135 sts along the cast-on edge, then fold the fabric in half so that the rev St st side is facing outward and needles are parallel. **Joining rnd** *Purl first st from front needle tog with first st from back needle; rep from * around. Cut yarn and put all 135 sts on waste yarn until they are needed for attaching a square.

Squares (brim)

Using dpns, work 9 first row squares (1 first row starting square, 7 first row middle squares, and 1 first row end square). Now work 9 second row squares. Put all 135 sts from the top edges of the second row squares onto the circular needle (see Note). Using A, knit 1 rnd, purl 1 rnd, then knit 4 rnds.

Crown shaping

Change to dpns when you have too few sts to fit comfortably on your circular needle.
Rnd 1 [K2tog, k13] 9 times—126 sts.
Rnd 2 and all even rnds Knit.
Rnd 3 [K6, k2tog, k6] 9 times—117 sts.
Rnd 5 [K11, k2tog] 9 times—108 sts.
Rnd 7 [K5, k2tog, k5] 9 times—99 sts.
Rnd 9 [K2tog, k9] 9 times—90 sts.
Rnd 11 [K2tog, k3] 18 times—72 sts.
Rnd 13 [K2tog, k2] 18 times—54 sts.
Rnd 15 [K2tog, k1] 18 times—36 sts.
Rnd 17 Using E, [k2tog] 18 times—18 sts. Cut yarn and thread through the rem sts. Pull tight to close the hole, then secure the yarn end on the inside of the hat. With a tapestry needle, weave in loose yarn tails to the WS of work and secure. Block the edge if needed.

INSTRUCTIONS FOR THE GLOVES

Anchor piece

Using A, CO 45 sts. Work in St st for 1"/2.5cm. Using spare needles, pick up and k45 sts along the cast-on edge, then fold the fabric in half so that the rev St st side is facing outward and needles from the two edges are parallel. **Joining rnd** *Purl first st from front needle tog with first st from back needle; rep from * around. Cut the yarn and put all 45 sts on waste yarn until they are needed for attaching a square.

Squares (cuff)

Work 3 first row squares (1 first row starting square, 1 first row middle square, and 1 first row end square). *There is no second row of squares.* Hand-pick one of the points where two squares meet to be your center palm point. (The way that the stitches are arranged on the needles is important as it ensures that a single square will be centered on the back of the wrist when the gloves are worn.)

Needle setup

Hold the glove so that the center back point is facing you. **For right glove** Put the 12 sts to the right of the center back point on one needle and put 11 sts on each of three other needles. **For left glove** Put the 12 sts to the left of the center back point onto one needle and put 11 sts on each of three other needles. The needle with 12 sts on it is N3 (counting clockwise) for the purposes of foll the instructions below. Attach A between N1 and N2. Knit 1 rnd, purl 1 rnd, then knit 4 rnds.

Thumb gusset

Next rnd N1 and N2: K22; N3: M1, k1, M1, knit to end; N4: K11. Knit 3 rnds.
Next rnd N1 and N2: K22; N3: M1, k3, M1, knit to end. N4: K11. Knit 3 rnds. Cont in this manner, inc 2 sts on N3 every 4th rnd (with the M1's occuring at the beg of the needle and after the previous number of center sts plus 2) until there are 26 sts on N3—59 sts total.

Thumb

Next rnd K37; put rem 22 sts and the first 22 sts of rnd on waste yarn—15 thumb sts rem. Using dpns, CO 1 st, and purl 1 rnd. *Using B, knit 2 rnds. Using A, knit 1 rnd, then purl 1 rnd. Using C, knit 2 rnds. Using A, knit 1 rnd, then purl 1 rnd. Using D, knit 2 rnds. Using A, knit 1 rnd, then purl 1 rnd. Using E, knit 2 rnds. BO *loosely.* * Put the 44 hand sts back on the dpns (11 on each needle). *The point at which you started the thumb is now the beg of the rnd.* Attach A, pick up and k 1 st at base of thumb, knit to end of rnd, pick up and k 1 st at base of thumb—46 sts total. Knit for 1"/2.5cm.

Little finger

K18, put these sts and the last 18 sts on waste yarn—10 little finger sts rem. Using dpns, knit these 10 sts, then CO 2 sts more and join—12 sts total. Purl 1 rnd, then rep from * to * as for thumb. Put the 36 hand sts back onto the dpns (9 on each needle). Using A, pick up and k 2 sts at point where you cast on 2 sts for the little finger. *The point between the 2 picked-up sts is now the beg of rnd.* Knit 4 rnds. Work the remaining fingers as folls:

Ring finger

K5, put the next 26 sts on waste yarn, CO 2 sts more, join rnd and k5—12 sts total. Purl 1 rnd, then rep from * to * as for thumb.

Middle finger

Put the first and last 6 sts from the waste yarn back onto the dpns. Using A, pick up and k2 sts at base of ring finger, k6, CO 2 sts more, k6—16 sts total. Purl 1 rnd, then rep from * to * as for thumb.

Index finger

Put the rem 14 sts back onto the dpns. Using A, CO 2 sts more. Purl 1 rnd, then rep from * to * as for thumb. With a tapestry needle, weave in loose yarn tails to the WS of work and secure.

INSTRUCTIONS FOR THE SOCKS

Anchor piece

Using larger dpns, A, and an elastic cast-on method, CO 60 sts. Join, taking care not to twist sts on needle. Pm to indicate beg of rnd and sl marker every rnd. Work in k1, p1 rib for 1¾"/4.5cm. Cut yarn and put all 45 sts on waste yarn until they are needed for attaching a square.

Squares (leg)

Using smaller dpns, make 4 first row squares (1 first row starting square, 2 first row middle squares, and 1 first row end square). Now work 4 second row squares.

Back heel

Slip 30 sts from 2 squares (see Note) onto smaller dpn and, with RS facing, attach A and knit 2 rows. Work in St st for ¾"/2cm.

Short-row heel

This technique for making short-row heels/toes was developed by Priscilla Gibson-Roberts.
Row 1 Knit to last st, turn.
Row 2 Wyib, insert RH needle into first st on LH needle and purl it. The yarn will come over the top of the RH needle and form a yo. Purl to last st; turn.
Row 3 Wyif, insert RH into first st on LH needle and knit it. The yarn will again come over the top of the RH needle and form a yo. Knit to the st before the yo, turn.
Row 4 Yo, purl to the st before the yo, turn.
Row 5 Yo, knit to the st before the yo, turn. Cont

in this manner until there are 10 sts between yo's, end with a WS row.

Turn the heel

Next row (RS) Knit to the first yo; insert RH needle into yo *k-wise* and slip it to RH needle (this will twist the yo so that it sits differently on the needle). Slip the twisted yo back to LH needle and knit it together with next st, turn.

Next row Yo, purl to the first yo; insert RH needle *into the back* of the yo and slip it (twisting the yo); next, insert RH needle into st on LH needle *from the back* and slip it; slip both the twisted st and yo back to the LH needle and p2tog tbl; turn.

Next row Yo, knit to the 2 yo's and slip them one at a time *k-wise* to RH needle, then slip them back to LH; knit the yo's tog with the next st; turn.

Next row Yo, purl to the 2 yo's; insert RH needle *into the back* of each yo, one at a time, and slip them, then do the same for the subsequent st. Slip all 3 back to LH needle and p3tog tbl; turn. Cont in this manner until you have worked all the sts.

Instep

Using A and cont from heel, knit a 6¼"/16cm long sole. Cut the yarn, then place markers every 2"/5cm along both sides of the sole. The instep will be filled in with 3 rows of instep squares, working first a right instep square, then a left square and then alternating right and left instep squares twice more.

Right instep square (make three)

Slip 15 sts from a previous square (square 1 from the leg, and squares 2 and 3 from right instep square) onto a needle. Using B, provisionally cast on 30 sts, then pick up and k15 sts along the edge of the sole, starting at one of the markers. Work as for first round starting square.

Left instep square (make three)

Slip 15 sts from the left (as it is facing you) cast-on edge of the right instep square last worked to a needle. Slip 15 sts from a previous square (square 1 from the leg, and squares 2 and 3 from left instep square) to a second needle. Using B, pick up and k15 sts along the edge of the sole, ending at one of the markers, then provisionally cast on 15 more sts. Work as for first round starting square.

HAND JIVE™

HAND JIVE IS THE SACRAMENTO-BASED BRAINCHILD of Darlene Hayes, a woman of many talents who retired from practicing law several years ago to start a knitting and design business. Darlene jokes that she has to change careers every decade or so or she gets bored. She knew it was time to leave the last one when she found herself wanting to spend more time backpacking and climbing mountains foraging for natural dyestuffs, than sitting in yet another contract meeting.

Now a designer who has featured garments in many of the leading knitting magazines, she also has her own business that sells patterns and naturally dyed yarns such as those used to create the items shown here. Visit Hand Jive at www.handjiveknits.com.

Toe

After you have filled in the instep, unravel any extra rows on the sole so that it is the same length as the instep. Put the 60 sole and instep sts on dpns, then using A, knit 1 rnd, then purl 1 rnd. Work even in St st until the foot measures 2"/5cm shorter than desired foot length. Work the toe foll the instructions for short-row heel above, starting with the stitches on the top of the foot. Graft the rem 30 toe sts to the sole sts. With a tapestry needle, weave in loose yarn tails to the WS of work and secure.

Taos Saltillo Jacket

DESIGNED BY JUDY DERCUM

Judy lives in Dillon, Colorado. She based this sweater on a traditional Spanish Saltillo design with a little alteration. The Saltillo pattern came to the New World from Spain; the Moors originally brought it there from Turkey. Judy used yarns from La Lana Wools in Taos, New Mexico; hence the name of the sweater. One of the West's signature flowers, Indian paintbrush, inspired the stranded band of flowers.

This colorful design calls for experience in intarsia and Fair Isle techniques.

Skill Level
Experienced

Sizes
Instructions are for Small. Changes for Medium, Large, and X-Large are in parentheses. Shown in size Medium.

Finished Measurements
Bust 43 (47, 51, 55)"/110 (119, 129, 140)cm

Length 27¼ (28, 29, 30)"/69 (71, 74, 76)cm

Yarn
PHAT SILK FINES by La Lana Wools, 2oz/57g skeins, each approx 71yd/65m (50% Bombyx silk/50% fine wool/3-light weight yarn)

• 5 (5, 6, 6) skeins in Indian Paintbrush (MC)

DOS MUJERES by La Lana Wools, 2oz/57g skeins, each approx 122yd/111.5m (55% mohair/45% merino wool) or a light weight yarn

• 1 skein in Medium Indigo Blue (A)

• 2 skeins in Fustic Yellow (B)

FOREVER RANDOM BLEND FINES by La Lana Wools, 2oz/57g skeins, each approx 118yd/108m (100% romney wool/3-light weight yarn)

• 2 skeins each in Sweet Lorraine (C) and Monet (D)

Needles & Notions
• Size 6 (4.25mm) circular needle, 32"/80cm long or size needed to obtain gauge

• Size 7 (4.5mm) circular needle, 24"/60cm long

• Size F/5 or G/6 (3.75 or 4mm) crochet hook

• Stitch holders

• Tapestry needle

Gauge
18 sts and 23 rows = 4"/10cm over St st using smaller needle.

A larger needle may be necessary to achieve correct gauge when working Fair Isle. Adjust the needle size as necessary to obtain correct gauge.

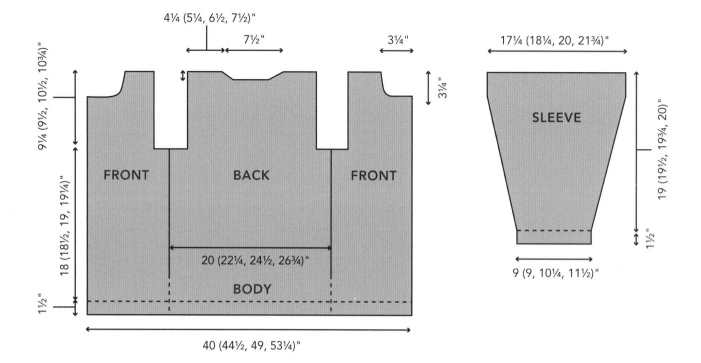

Construction Notes

1) This garment is worked from the bottom up, beginning with a hem and Fair Isle band, which goes around the entire bottom edge. At the knitter's discretion, this band can be worked in the round using steeks, then cut.

2) The stitches are then divided into back and fronts and each piece is worked separately in Intarsia.

3) The sleeves are also worked with a hem and Fair Isle band, followed by Intarsia. The bands are worked in Fair Isle and hemmed.

4) Instructions are given for optional pockets at the side seams.

GLOSSARY

※ **Fair Isle** This technique is worked using only 2 colors across the row; the yarn not being used is stranded loosely across the back of the fabric. To maintain the same gauge with the different knitting techniques in the garment, the pattern may direct the use of a larger needle for some of the Fair Isle portions.

※ **Intarsia** This technique requires a separate ball of yarn for each of the color blocks. To prevent holes in the fabric when changing from one color to the next, bring new yarn up from under old yarn, interlocking the two on the WS. Adjust the stitches to even up the join.

INSTRUCTIONS FOR JACKET

Bottom band

With smaller needle and MC, CO 182 (202, 222, 242) sts.

Hem and turning ridge

Beg with a RS row, work 9 rows in St st. Knit next 2 rows (turning ridge made). Charge to larger needle.

INTARSIA CHART

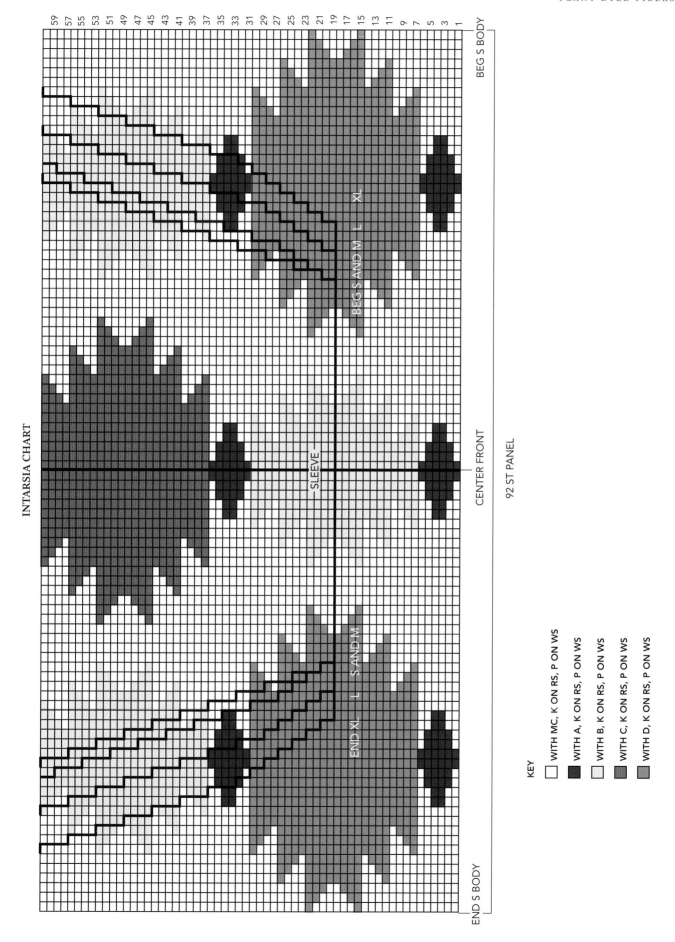

59 57 55 53 51 49 47 45 43 41 39 37 35 33 31 29 27 25 23 21 19 17 15 13 11 9 7 5 3 1

BEG S BODY

BEG S AND M-L-XL

SLEEVE

CENTER FRONT

92 ST PANEL

S AND M

L

END XL

END S BODY

KEY

☐ WITH MC, K ON RS, P ON WS

■ WITH A, K ON RS, P ON WS

☐ WITH B, K ON RS, P ON WS

▨ WITH C, K ON RS, P ON WS

▨ WITH D, K ON RS, P ON WS

Outer band

Next row K1 (selvedge) work 10-st Fair Isle rep (see Chart A) end K1 (selvedge). When 22 row chart is complete, slip the first and last 46 (51, 56, 61) sts on two holders for fronts.

Back

Place the back 90 (100, 110, 120) sts on smaller needle. CO 1 st each side for selvedge sts—92 (102, 112, 122) sts.

Next row With MC, k0 (5, 10, 15) sts, work Intarsia chart over next 92 sts, end k0 (5, 10, 15) with MC. Maintaining MC at side edges and working 60 row Intarsia chart, work even until

CHART A

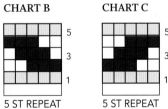

22
19
17
15
13
11
9
7
5
3
1

END L   XL   10 ST REPEAT   XL   L BEG
        S AND M   S AND M

CHART B   CHART C

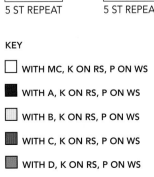

5   5
3   3
1   1

5 ST REPEAT   5 ST REPEAT

KEY

☐ WITH MC, K ON RS, P ON WS

■ WITH A, K ON RS, P ON WS

☐ WITH B, K ON RS, P ON WS

■ WITH C, K ON RS, P ON WS

■ WITH D, K ON RS, P ON WS

piece measures 18 (18½, 19, 19¼)"/46 (47, 48, 49)cm from turning ridge.

Armhole shaping

Maintaining pat, BO 10 sts at beg of next two rows—72 (82, 92, 102) sts. Cont working Intarsia chart and rep from Row 1 as necessary, work even until armhold measures 7¼ (8, 8¾, 9½)"/18.5 (20.5, 22, 24)cm, end with a WS row.

Neck shaping

Next row (RS) Maintaining pat, work across first 26 (31, 36, 41) sts, join a 2nd skein of yarn and BO center 20 sts, work to end. Working one side at a time, BO 3 sts at neck edge once, then 2 sts twice—19 (24, 29, 34) sts. Work even, if necessary, until arm measures 8½ (9¼, 10, 10¾)". BO all sts for shoulder. Re-join yarn to other side and work neck, reversing all shaping.

Left front

Slip sts for left front from holder to smaller needle. CO one st at side edge for selvedge—47 (52, 57, 62) sts.

Next row With MC, k0 (5, 10, 15) sts, beg at right edge of chart, work Intarsia chart to center, k1 selvedge in color being worked. Work even until piece measures same as back from turning ridge, end with a WS row.

Armhole shaping

Maintaining pat, BO 10 sts at beg of next row—37 (42, 47, 52) sts. Work even until armhole measures 5¼ (6, 6¾, 7½)"/13.5 (15, 17, 19) cm end with a RS row.

Neck shaping

Next row (WS) BO 9 sts, work to end. Dec 1 st at neck edge *every* row 5 times, every other row twice, then every 4th row twice—19 (24, 29, 34) sts. Work even until front measures same as back to shoulder. Bind off all sts.

Right front

Slip sts for right front from holder onto *smaller* needle. CO 1 st at side edge for selvedge. Beg at center of chart, cont to work as for left front, reversing all shaping.

Sleeves

With smaller needle and MC, CO 42 (42, 48, 54) sts.

LA LANA WOOLS

LOCATED IN TAOS, NEW MEXICO, LA LANA WOOLS IS THE CREATION OF LUISA GELENTER.

As soon as you walk into the store, you will see that she has maximized Mother Nature's colors and created a mecca for yarn aficionados. All her yarns are dyed with plants and everything goes together wonderfully. Luisa has created a beautiful collection of colors. Some of her yarns are handspun and some are millspun.

Luisa fell in love with spinning in Bolivia in the early 1970s. She refers to those days as dancing with wool! In addition to experimenting with a variety of plant dyes, she also experiments with a variety of spinning techniques and combinations of fibers. For instance, she has a line of yarn called Forever Random Blends. In this collection, there is no set color pattern. The colors occur as the spinner uses them, and there is always a changing color—which makes for an interesting yarn and knitting experience!

Hem and turning ridge rows
Beg with a RS row, work 9 rows in St st. Knit next 2 rows for turning ridge. Change to larger needle.

Outer band
Next row K1 (selvedge) beg Chart A where indicated for Fair Isle pat, k1 (selvedge). Work even until 22–row chart is complete.
Next row Working first and last sts as selvedge sts in color being worked at edges, k1 (selvedge), work Intarsia chart, beg where indicated for size for sleeve, end k1 (selvedge). AT THE SAME TIME, maintaining pat (rep Intersia chart from Row 1 as necessary), inc 1 st each side every other row 1 (4, 5, 7) times, then every 4th row 18 (18, 17, 16) times—80 (86, 92, 100) sts. Work even until piece measures approx 19 (19½, 19¾, 20)"/ #48 (49, 50, 51)cm from turning ridge, or desired length, end with a WS row. BO all sts *loosely*.

FINISHING

With a tapestry needle, weave in loose yarn tails to the WS of work and secure. Wet-block pieces to measurements. Sew shoulder seams.

Front bands
Outer band With RS facing, using smaller needle and MC, pick up and k90 (95, 100, 105) sts evenly spaced along left front edge. Change to *larger* needle and work Chart B.
Turning ridge and hem Change to smaller needle and MC, knit 2 rows (turning ridge made), then work 9 rows St st. Using *larger* needle, BO all sts *loosely*. Rep for right front, working Chart C.

Neckband
Outer band With RS facing, using smaller needle and MC, pick up and k36 sts along right front neck edge, 46 sts along back neck edge, then 36 sts along left front neck edge—118 sts. Change to larger needle and work first row of Chart B, dec 3 sts evenly spaced along back neck edge—115 sts. Complete Chart B.
Turning ridge and hem Change to smaller needle and MC and knit next 2 rows (turning ridge made), then work 9 rows in St st. BO all sts *loosely*. Turn each hem to WS along turning ridge and sew BO edge in place. Set in sleeves. Sew side (see optional pocket, *below*) and sleeve seams.

Optional pocket (make 2)
Beg 4½"/11.5cm from bottom turning ridge, leave a 6"/15cm opening in the side seams. With *smaller* needle and MC, pick up and k 30 sts along back edge of pocket opening. Work even in St st for 1"/2.5cm, then inc 1 st at bottom edge *every* row 4 times, then every other row twice—36 sts. Work 4 rows even, then dec 1 st at bottom edge every other row 4 times. BO all sts. Push pocket to inside of garment and slip st in place. With *smaller needle* and MC, pick up and k 30 sts along front edge of pocket opening. Knit 1 row. BO all sts. Sew in ends.

Think Zinnias!

DESIGNED BY ANNA ZILBOORG

When it comes to covering the extremities, Anna Zilboorg is known for creating boldly colored hats, socks, and mittens such as the pair that you see here. These festive and functional mittens beg to be part of a snowball fight! There is no guarantee that your snowball will hit its target, but at least these mittens will protect your wrists from the snow that usually sneaks into the vulnerable space between the top of your mittens and your jacket. Anna said that she made these mittens in black with glitzy gold patterning for use as evening mittens.

Made with a corriedale and romney mix wool yarn from Snow Star Farm, the yarn was spun using a "green" process (that is, without petroleum). Traditional dyestuffs and plant materials gathered from around the farm create these brilliant colors.

Unlike many mitten patterns, Anna works each mitten from the tip to the cuff and inserts an invisible thumb. Make two identical mittens as shown here, or mix things up and switch two of the colors to make mittens that coordinate.

Skill Level
Experienced

Size
Instructions are for women's size Medium.

Finished Measurements
Gloves
Hand circumference 6¾"/17cm

Length from wrist to top 7½"/19cm

Yarn
SNOW STAR FARM YARN, 4oz/113.5g skeins, each approx 270yd/247m (100% corriedale/romney woo) or a medium weight yarn

• 1 skein each in Cochineal Rose (A), Madder Orange (B) and Indigo Navy (C) or 2oz/57g each in Cochineal Rose (A) and Madder Orange (B) and 1oz/28.5g in Indigo Navy (C)

Needles & Notions
• One set (5) size 4 (3.5mm) double-pointed needles (dpns) *or size needed to obtain gauge*

• Waste yarn for stitch holders

• Tapestry needle

Gauge
26 sts and 25 rnds = 4"/10cm over 2-color pat worked in the round using size 4 (3.5mm) dpns.

Adjust the needle sizes as necessary to obtain correct gauge.

Double Knot Embroidery Stitch

Step 1: Bring needle up from WS, then back down to WS a short distance away (forming a diagonal line on RS), then back up to RS.

Step 2: Slide needle under left side of diagonal line. Do not go through fabric.

Step 3: Slide needle under right side of diagonal line, bringing needle OVER the yarn. Pull gently to form knot.

Step 4: Take needle to WS. Come back up in position desired and begin again from Step 1.

Construction Notes

1) These mittens are worked from the top down with 2-color stranding, Fair Isle style, and 5 double-pointed needles.

2) The thumb is worked first, then put on hold; the mitten top is worked next and the thumb is joined using 3-needle bindoff.

3) The wrist and cuff are worked last, ending with I-cord fringe.

4) Double knots are embroidered on the mitten back after it is finished.

GLOSSARY

M1 Inc 1 by placing twisted loop on RH needle.

N1, N2, N3, N4 Needle 1, Needle 2, Needle 3, Needle 4.

3-needle bindoff Holding needles parallel with RS together and WS facing, k2tog from front and back needles, *k2tog from front and back needles and pass the first st over the second to bind off; rep from * to end.

INSTRUCTIONS FOR THE MITTENS

Thumb setup

With A, using the half-hitch (back loop, e-wrap) cast-on, CO 4 sts. Turn needle as if to knit, then rotate the needle so that the bottom of the sts is on top. With another needle, pick up and k the 3 loops that run along the bottom. Turn the work so that you can knit the cast-on sts. Drop the first st, then with another needle, knit the rem 3 sts. On the same 3 sts, purl 1 row, then knit 1 row.

Rnd 1 *With another needle, pick up and k 2 sts on the side of the rectangle. With another needle, knit the 3 end sts; rep from * around—10 sts on 4 needles.

Rnd 2 *K1, M1; rep from * around—20 sts. Work thumb chart and place sts on a waste yarn holder.

Top

With B, using the half-hitch cast-on, CO 5 sts. Turn needle as if to knit, then rotate it so that the bottom of the stitches is on top. With another needle, pick up and k the 4 loops that run along the bottom. Turn. *Purl 1 row, knit 1 row; rep from * twice more.

Rnd 1 With another needle (N2) and A, pick up and k 5 sts along the side of the rectangle (pick up under both legs of the sts); then drop the end loop off the cast-on needle (N3) and with another needle and B, knit across these sts (you may have to knit through the back of the loops in order not to twist the sts); with another needle (N4) and A, pick up and k 5 sts along the other side of the rectangle; with B and another needle, knit the original 4 sts (N1)—4 sts B on N1 and N3; 5 sts A on N2 and N4.

Rnd 2 Work another rnd, picking up 1 st at the beg and end of N2 and N4.

(**Note** Some knitters have trouble knowing where to pick up these stitches. Look at it this way: if you had not picked up stitches, but had knit two more rows on the rectangle, you would have had two more rows in which to pick up stitches. By working around, you have knit another row on each of the orange (side) needles. So you have another row at each end of the red (back and palm) needles in which to pick up stitches.)

Beg working chart pat. Cont picking up sts and foll chart until there are 23 sts on N2 and N4.

Dec rnd N1: K 3 sts; N2: Place the last st of N1 on N2 and knit it tog with first st on N2, then work pat foll chart to last st, ssk last st tog with first st on N3; N3: K2; N4: Knit the last st of N2 tog with the first st on N4, then work pat, foll chart to last st, ssk the last st tog with the first st on N1—50 sts (2 sts on N1 and N2, 23 sts on N2 and N4). Cont around in pat (feel free to rearrange sts on needles) until you reach the line on the chart that marks the base of the thumb.

Insert thumb

Divide the thumb sts on 2 needles, each holding half the sts constituting the back and the front of the thumb. Line these sts up with the mitten sts on either the right or left side of the palm (depending on whether you're making the right or left hand). Line them up with RS tog with the tip of the thumb pointing to the tip of the mitten. Work 3-needle bindoff, joining the mitten sts with the inside thumb sts. Replace the bound off mitten sts with the rem thumb sts. Complete chart and cut B.

Ribbed wrist

With A, knit 1 rnd.

Next rnd *K1tbl, p1, k1tbl, p2tog; rep from* around—40 sts.

LEFT THUMB CHART

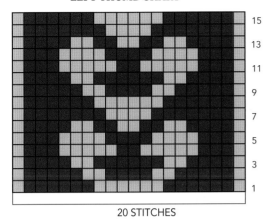

15
13
11
9
7
5
3
1

20 STITCHES

RIGHT THUMB CHART

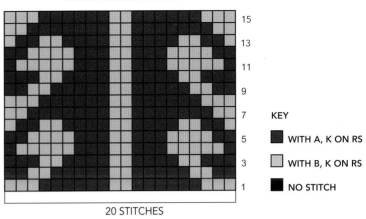

15
13
11
9
7
5
3
1

KEY

■	WITH A, K ON RS
▢	WITH B, K ON RS
■	NO STITCH

20 STITCHES

MITTEN CHART

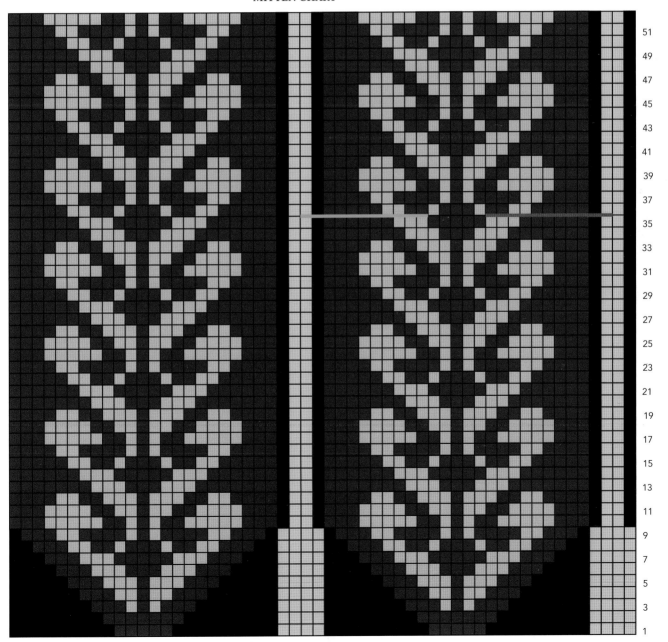

51
49
47
45
43
41
39
37
35
33
31
29
27
25
23
21
19
17
15
13
11
9
7
5
3
1

SNOW STAR FARM

AT SNOW STAR FARM, LORANNE CAREY BLOCK BELIEVES IN "KEEPING TRADITIONS ALIVE BY doing it in the old way."

On her small New Hampshire family farm, sheep are raised naturally without hormones or chemicals, and they graze only on organic pasture. Sheep breeds have been selected specifically for their inherent wool characteristics: corriedale for softness, and romney for staple length, luster, and strength.

Using only the best parts of the fleece, the resulting natural wool is carefully blade-shorn and custom-spun to exacting specifications into two- and three-ply knitting yarns with a firm twist. The yarn is then dyed in small batches at the Block home, using traditional dyestuffs and plant materials found on the Block farm.

Although this is certainly a time-consuming process, it's a labor that expresses Loranne's care and concern for the natural environment.

Next 4 rnds Work k1tbl, p1 rib.

Last rnd *K1b, p2 in next st; rep from * around—60 sts.

Cuff

Knot st pat

Rnd 1 With B, * (k1, yo, k1) in the next st, sl 1; rep from * around.

Rnd 2 With B, *p3tog (the k1, yo and k1), sl 1 wyif; rep from * around.

Rnds 3–6 With C, knit.

Rnds 7 and 8 With A, rep Rnds 1 and 2.

Rnds 9–11 With C, knit.

Rnd 12 With C, knit, inc 8 sts evenly spaced around—68 sts. Rep Rnds 1–12 twice more, then

Rnds 1–8 once—total of 8 knot st stripes.

I-cord fringe

With C, * [k3, slip the 3 sts back onto LH needle] 5 times; cut yarn, thread onto tapestry needle and run yarn through the 3 sts, pulling tight. Run yarn through tube to its base and cut off—one I-cord fringe made; rep from * around, joining new length of C for each fringe. Run beg yarn ends through their tubes and cut off at top.

FINISHING

Embroider back of mitten with double knot stitch as shown. With a tapestry needle, weave in loose yarn tails to the WS of work and secure.

Lucky Fish Mini Case

DESIGN BY JENNIFER LINDSAY

Use this little case to carry your music player in style wherever you go. These cases make wonderful little wardrobe accessories and great gifts for the music lovers in your life! The fingering weight of Nature's Palette yarn lends itself well to the fine detail and the small size of the finished piece.

Find your own motif and experiment with colors and designs to customize your very own.

Skill Level
Easy

Finished Measurements
4¼" x 3"/10.5cm x 7.5cm

Yarn
FINGERING WEIGHT YARN by Nature's Palette™, 1¾oz/50g skeins, each approx 185yd/169m (100% washable merino wool) or super fine weight yarn
• 1 skein each in NP-134 Coral Bells (MC) and NP-122 Spring Grass (CC)

Needles & Notions
• One set (5) each of sizes 0 and 1 (2 and 2.25mm) double-pointed needles (dpns) *or size needed to obtain gauge*
• Scraps of tapestry wool or embroidery floss in various blues and greens for motif (Suggestions: Paternyan Persian yarn or DMC Floss; since very little yarn shows in the motif, it doesn't really matter what color you use, as long as it works with your beads.)
• Two coil-less safety pins or split-ring markers
• Bead threader
• Tapestry needle

Beads
Size 6/0 seed beads for lucky fish motif and other decorations
• Twenty-eight Turquoise Luster for tail fins
• Fourteen Green Iris Rainbow for fish head
• Thirty-seven Light Olivine Copper Lined for fish body and bottom edge of bag
• Thirty-three Silver Lined Mix for side fins (light and dark versions of the azure color) and top edge (mixed colors)
Other beads
• Two Turkish Blue Eyes for fish eyes
• Two Bright Blue Venetian glass beads for tassels
• Two Yellow jade circles for tassels

Gauge
32 sts and 34 rnds = 4"/10cm over St st using larger needles.
Adjust the needle size as necessary to obtain correct gauge.

Construction Notes

1) This case is worked in the round on double-pointed needles from bottom to top.

2) At the top, a picot turning edge is worked, followed by a facing that is sewn to the inside.

3) The lucky fish design is done in beaded duplicate stitch (after the case is knitted and before sewing the bottom seam) using size 6/0 colored seed beads that are threaded onto tapestry yarn or embroidery floss.

4) Turkish glass beads with the traditional symbol of a blue eye, a talisman to protect the wearer against bad luck, create the fish's eyes.

GLOSSARY

⬚ **Beaded duplicate stitch** Thread a tapestry needle with a length of single-ply tapestry yarn or embroidery floss in the color of your choice. From the inside of the work, push the needle up through the fabric at the base of a knit stitch, leaving an end of about 1"–2"/2.5–5cm inside the case to tie off later. Change the tapestry needle to a bead threader, and thread one bead onto the yarn. Change back to the tapestry needle. Following the outline of the stitch, thread the yarn through both legs of the stitch above and then back down into the hole where you started. Repeat for each stitch of the motif, changing colors of beads and tapestry yarns as necessary for effect. Tie off ends on back of work.

INSTRUCTIONS FOR MINI CASE

Case

With larger dpns and MC, CO 40 sts. Join, taking care not to twist sts on needle; pm for beg of rnd. Knit 41 rnds.

Next rnd Knit, placing a safety pin or split-ring marker on st 20 and st 40 to mark side seams. Purl 1 rnd. Change to CC and smaller needles. Knit 5 rows.

Next (picot edge) rnd * K2tog, yo; rep from * around. Knit 4 rnds for facing. BO all sts using larger dpn. Fold facing and sew it to the inside of the case.

I-Cord edging and strap

Fold case flat with markers at the left and right sides. With the placement of marker as a guide and using smaller needles and a 10"/25.5cm length of CC, pick up and k 38 sts in the horizontal running threads along the "seam" or fold line on the left side of the case, stopping (or starting) at the purl row that defines the color change at the top edge.

Attach I-cord to side of case

Work a 3-st applied I-cord along the left side edge as folls: Beg at bottom of case with picked-up sts on the LH needle. Using a second needle and CC

DUPLICATE STITCH AND BEADING CHART

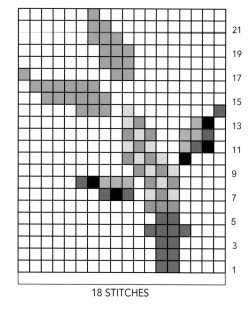

18 STITCHES

⬚ TURQUOISE LUSTER BEAD

⬚ BLUE YARN - NO BEAD

⬚ LIGHT AZURE BEAD

⬛ DARK AZURE BEAD

⬚ GREEN YARN - NO BEAD

⬚ LIGHT OLIVENE BEAD

⬚ GREEN IRIS BEAD

from ball, cable CO 3 sts onto LH needle. Knit the first 2 of the CO sts, then ssk the 3rd st and the first of the 38 sts picked up along the side of the case. *DO NOT TURN. Slip 3 sts back to LH needle, k2, ssk; rep from * until you have joined all 38 sts to cord and 3 sts rem on needle. Work strap as folls: K2, M1, k1 (you now have a 4-st I-cord). *DO NOT TURN. Slip the 4 sts back to LH needle, k4; rep from *. When cord measures 29"/73.5cm, or desired length, dec 1 st (you now have a 3-st I-cord). Attach I-cord to other side of bag. Using a separate needle, pick up and k 38 sts along opposite side of case, and work attached I-cord as before, starting at the marker just below the purl stitch edging and working to the bottom edge. When all 38 sts have been attached to I-cord, BO the 3 I-cord sts.

FINISHING

With a tapestry needle, weave in loose yarn tails to the WS of work and secure. Decorate case with lucky fish motif, foll Chart and directions for beaded duplicate stitch, or design your own embroidered motif. After motif is complete, sew bottom of case closed using about 10"/25cm of yarn in MC and an overcast seam, threading a bead onto the yarn between each stitch, so that beads decorate bottom edge of case. Neaten and close up edges where the trim meets the body of the bag. Using a bead as an anchor, secure the strap to each side of case at the purl stitch edging.

Tassels or other ornaments

Use any sort of decorative ornaments that capture your fancy. Here, ends from the knitting at the bottom corners of the case were threaded through glass beads using a bead threader, wound around two open yellow jade circlets, and then were passed back though the bead and tied off inside the case. In addition, beads were placed between each picot point at the top edge of the case. To do this, use a short length of yarn and a tapestry or bead needle. Tie it to one side seam inside the case. Run the yarn along the top edge of the case, placing a bead on the yarn between each picot point. Do not pull the thread too tightly, but make sure the beads sit securely between the points. Tie off the ends inside the case.

A Natural Dye Shortcut: Earthues

For those who don't want to go foraging for plant dyes, there are plant dye extracts (shown in powdered form, above). Michele Wipplinger's company, Earthues, offers a range of nontoxic natural dye extracts that yield brilliant, consistent, and lightfast hues. Michelle, a master dyer and educator, has traveled the world sourcing dyestuffs.

Committed to working with artisans of other cultures, Michele frequently consults worldwide with both governmental and NGO groups to support the revival of and innovation in traditional textiles and crafts. She also works with cottage industries and cooperatives to develop markets for natural dyestuffs that sustain rural populations and respect these peoples' local resources.

Chapter 5
NATURAL NEXT STEPS

So you are a knitter. Perhaps you want to take one step back, closer to the sheep, and become a spinner? Most people learn to knit first. After all, you can easily purchase knitting needles and yarn, and they are quite portable.

It's a little bit more difficult to come by a spinning wheel, though more than one knitter has purchased a wheel to add a homespun look to her home and soon became addicted to spinning.

When you spin your own yarn, you can learn to make the yarn of your dreams. For instance, wool is elastic and matte in finish. Mohair can be lustrous and heavy, and, when used alone, can result in knitted items that bag out and sag. But when these two fibers are blended together, they can create a yarn that makes the most of both qualities, luster and ease.

The sky is the limit as far as what you can mix and match. But wool is the easiest fiber to begin with. First you have to find the fiber, which is available directly from sheep farms or sometimes sold already cleaned and processed, which is called roving. Wool is available in many forms, depending on how much work you want to do to prepare the yarn.

If the wool comes directly from the sheep, wash it by soaking it in hot water in a washing machine with a non-petroleum based detergent, such as Ecover. (Do not agitate.) Spin to remove water and detergent. Fill the machines again with hot water and rinse the wool. Spin to remove water, and repeat as needed. The wool can then be air-dryed or placed in a garment bag for air-drying in the dryer. It is important that the temperature of the wool remain consistent throughout the process, as any sudden changes may cause it to felt. When dry, use carders to separate and align the fibers, pulling out any small, loose fibers. Then the wool will be ready to be spun into yarn. For handspinning, you can use a drop spindle or a spinning wheel.

If you are a knitting store "junkie" and don't hang out with spinners, take a look around and you will probably find a spinner among the fiber goddesses you know! Even if you are not interested in spinning, perhaps you can work out a deal: she spins you the yarn of your dreams, and you in turn knit something for her using her handspun goods.

The fiber possibilities are endless! There is a whole natural world out there that you might not have noticed before. See how you can now take control over your own yarn creation.

Next stop on the fiber trail—becoming a shepherd/shepherdess!

Opposite
A spinner is shown drafting un-spun fiber onto a spinning wheel.

Crimp

Crimp is another characteristic of fiber that will affect how the spun fiber behaves. Crimp is the reoccurrence of corrugation in a fiber. In the book **The Alden Amos Big Book of Handspinning**, Alden says that classifying yarn by crimp—as in more crimps per unit of length, or the more uniform the distribution of the crimps—the higher the quality of the wool. Luis Chavez, who is in charge of purchasing and processing alpaca fiber for Grupo Inca in Peru, says in Alpacas magazine, "If you have a small box filled with coiled springs made of the same diameter wire as a similar box filled with straight pieces of the same wire, the box filled with the springs will be lighter." The argument here is that a fine-crimped fiber can allow for a lighter-weight yarn to be spun.

The Felted Bead Diva's Flowers

DESIGN BY CAROL CYPHER

"When I reveal to knitters that I am a felt maker, they frequently tell me about the hat or tote they felted, by first knitting and then laundering or 'shrinking' the item in hot soapy water. (At the peril of sounding nit-picky, these beautiful items are actually fulled, not felted.) Consider the instant gratification of creating an item directly from wool without having to spin it into yarn and knit it into fabric, says Carol. "Indulge in the spontaneity, creative possibilities and painterly approach of working with a rich palette of dyed wool. This easy and accessible technique for feltmaking will show you how, and you'll have a felt flower to wear on your lapel or hat. Embellish it with beads, or not."

Skill Level
Easy

Finished Measurements
4" x 4"/10 x 10cm to
8" x 8"/20 x 20cm

Wool
PLANT DYED SOLIDS by La Lana Wools (100% wool fiber)

• 1oz/28g each in Goldenrod/Grey (A), Cochineal Sweet Pea (C), Puesta del Sol (D) and Brazilwood (E)

FOREVER RANDOM BLENDS by La Lana Wools (100% romney wool and wool/mohair blends)

• 1oz/28g each in TeRosada (B), Deep Sea Indigo (F), Spiced Mullein (G) and Potpourri (H)

Or
• If using wool from your stash, choose a wool you know will felt easily, such as merino. Use 3 to 5 colors per flower, totaling ¾/22g to 1oz/28g of fiber per flower.

Equipment
• 12"/30.5cm square of bubble wrap

• 12"/30.5cm square of high density plastic (veg/market bag that rustles when touched)

• Retired knee high or pantyhose leg

• Small towel

• 12"/30.5cm length of pipe insulation

• Six drops of dishwashing liquid in 2 cups/0.25 liter hot water

• Dowel, pencil, or skewer

• Styrofoam balls in small sizes

Notions
• Scissors

• Beading needle

• Nymo beading thread

• Assorted seed beads

• Straight pins

• Safety pin

INSTRUCTIONS FOR FLOWER

Arrange the wool in flower formation.

Place bubble wrap on your work surface, smooth side up.

Lay color A in a 5-petal design on the smooth side of the bubble wrap.

Cover color A with ¼oz/7g of color H in a solid circle design of 6"/15cm to 8"/20cm diameter.

Pull little wisps of color E off and lay them side by side in rows to cover the circle; add a second layer of color E with the fiber running perpendicular to the first (total of approx ½oz/14g color E).

Finish with less than a ¼oz/7g of color H, laying out the fiber in a painterly approach, radiating from the center.

Setup for felting

Sprinkle the wool with ½ cup/.25 liter of hot soapy water.

Cover with the high density plastic.

Press down on the plastic with one hand and press and spread the water throughout the wool with the other hand without moving the plastic or wool beneath it. Your mission is to simply press out the air and wet down every fiber of wool to facilitate felting.

Place the pipe insulation on one edge and roll up the bubble wrap/wool/plastic layers. Secure the tightly rolled bundle with a knee high or pantyhose leg. Do not knot. An easy alternative is to tie once very tightly, then switch the direction of your grasp and without adding another tie, just pull hard.

Felt the wool

Using both hands extended out flat, roll the bundle back and forth about a hundred times. Keep a towel convenient to mop up water leakage when roll is squeezed.

Unroll, move pipe insulation to a 2nd of the 4 edges, reroll, and tie. Roll back and forth a hundred times.

Repeat for all 4 edges.

Shape the flower

Unroll the bundle and take out the flower. How do you want to shape it? Use as is for a poppy look. Cut into 4 or 5 petals or slash several times for a mum look. Make sure that petals are not cut off or cut too thin.

Reroll and tie the bundle again; roll it a hundred times to eliminate the cut-edge look. Separate the petals if they are felting together. Reroll, tie, and roll it back and forth again.

Now consider the dimensional appearance of the flower. Poke a pencil, skewer, or dowel in the center. Allow the flower to drape over the tip like an umbrella. Tie the bundle this way and work it for 2 or 3 rounds of rolling it back and forth 150 times.

Rinse under hot water. Shape the flower as desired and maintain the shape by sticking straight pins into Styrofoam ball. Allow the water to drain by holding the flower vertically.

Optional Sprinkle Mop and Glo or Future floor "wax" onto the felt flower. Allow it to dry. This serves as an acrylic medium, lending the flower body but not making it too stiff to push a bead needle through.

Embellish the flower

Use seed beads to embellish your flower, creating stamens or adding dense spots of light and shine to the matte softness of the felt.

Attach beads using embroidery stitches or fringe techniques or simply sew one bead on at a time.

Alternate flower recipes

Start with 5 petals of color A and make layers of color C finished with color D.

Start with 5 petals of color A and make layers of color F finished with color H.

Design ideas

Use the safety pin to wear the flower on your lapel, hat, or purse. Consider using it as part of a floral arrangement, as a curtain tie-back, or as a pillow adornment.

ABBREVIATIONS AND TECHNIQUES

[ ]   work instructions within brackets as many times as directed

( )   work instructions within parentheses in the place directed

*   repeat instructions following the single asterisk as directed

**   repeat instructions following the asterisks as directed

"   inch(es)

approx	approximately	p2tog	purl 2 stitches together
beg	begin(ning)	p-wise	purlwise
BO	bind off	rem	remain(ing)
CO	cast on	rep	repeat(s)
CC	contrasting color	rev St st	reverse stockinette stitch
cm	centimeter(s)	RH	right hand
cn	cable needle	rnd(s)	round(s)
cont	continue(ing)	RS	right side
dec	decrease(s)(ing)	sl	slip
dpn(s)	double-pointed needle(s)	sl st	slip stitch: An unworked stitch made by passing a stitch from LH needle to RH needle as if to purl
foll(s)	follow(s)(ing)		
g	gram(s)	ssk	slip, slip, knit these 2 stitches together (a left-leaning decrease)
inc	increase(s)(ing)		
k	knit	sssk	slip, slip, slip, knit 3 stitches together
k2tog	knit 2 stitches together	st(s)	stitch(es)
k-wise	knitwise	St st	stockinette stitch
LH	left hand	tbl	through back loop
m	meter(s)	tog	together
M1	Make 1: Insert LH needle under the horizontal thread between the stitch just worked and the next st and k into the back of it.	WS	wrong side
		wyib	with yarn in back
		wyif	with yarn in front
MC	main color	yd(s)	yard(s)
mm	millimeter(s)	yo	yarn over
oz	ounce(s)		
p	purl		
pat	pattern(s)		
pm	place marker		
psso	pass slipped stitch over		

KNITTING & YARN RESOURCES

KNITTING RESOURCES

knittersreview.com
In the how-to section of this website, Clara Parkes covers a variety of topics from natural dyeing to yarn substitutions.

knitting.about.com
This website has numerous tutorials to get you going and help you with finishing techniques.

knittinghelp.com
Free video downloads cover basic and advanced techniques, including several cast-on methods, color knitting, and grafting.

knitty.com
Great features, like one on steeking, abound in this monthly magazine.

learntoknit.com
Sponsored by the CYCA, this is a good place to start if you need help with the very basics.

YARN RESOURCES

Aurora Silk
5806 North Vancouver Avenue
Portland, OR 97217
503-286-4149
Fax: 503-286-6247
www.aurorasilk.com

Naturally dyed fiber products, as well as natural dyes, books, articles, and workshops on natural dyeing, as well as silk fiber, cocoons, and silkworms.

Beadazzled
1507 Connecticut Avenue NW
Washington, DC 20016
202-265-2323
www.beadazzled.net
Beads, textiles, gifts.

Blue Sky Alpaca
PO Box 387
St. Francis, MN 55070
763-753-5815
Toll Free: 888-460-8862
www.blueskyalpacas.com
email: sylvia@blueskyalpacas.com

Alpaca and alpaca blend yarns and organic cotton yarn.

Botanical Shades (formerly Tregellys Fibers and Shades)
Tregellys Fiber Farm
15 Doge Branch Road
Hawley, MA 01339
413-625-9492
Yarns hand-dyed with natural botanical dyes.

Bufcufs (aka Cottonwood)
204 South Laird Street
White Pigeon, MI 49099
269-483-2445
email: bufcufs@myrural.com
Washed and carded buffalo fiber, yarn, felting bats, roving, handmade items.

California Cashmere Company
PO Box 1030
San Andreas, CA 95249 USA
209-754-5751
Fax: 209-754-1044
Toll Free: 866-754-5751
www.calcashmere.com
Cashmere fiber, fleece, yarn, and livestock.

Classic Elite Yarns
122 Western Avenue
Lowell, MA 01851-1434
978-453-2837
Fax: 978-452-3085
www.classiceliteyarns.com
Fine hand-knitting yarns, accessories, patterns, and related products for the creative hand-knitter, crocheter, and weaver.

David Reed Smith
1706 Mar Sue Drive
Hampstead MD 21074-1115
410-374-5318
www.davidreedsmith.com
Handcrafted spindles, niddy noddys, and other fiber accessories.

Goldings
Meadowsweet Farm Icelandics
849 Saxtons River Road
Saxtons River, VT 05154
Toll Free: 800-710-1872
www.dropspindle.info
Beautiful handcrafted drop spindles, spinning wheels, looms, and supplies.

Green Mountain Spinnery
PO Box 568
Putney, VT 05346
802-387-4528
Fax: 802-387-4841
Toll Free: 800-321-9665
www.spinnery.com
email: spinnery@sover.net
Yarn and knitting supplies.

Habu Textiles
135 West 29th Street, Suite 804
New York, NY 10001
212-239-3546
www.habutextiles.com
email: habu.textiles@verizon.net
Contemporary and traditional Japanese fibers and yarns, natural and plant dyed.

Hand Jive Knits
3325 Cutter Way
Sacramento, CA 95818
916-806-8063
www.handjiveknits.com
email: darlenehayes@handjiveknits.com
Nature's Palette™ yarn, patterns, and kits.

Haneke Merino Wools
4600 Quarterhorse Lane
Meridian, ID 83642
208-888-6934
Toll Free: 800-523-WOOL
www.hanekewoolfashions.com
Yarn producer, processor, and retailer.

Harrisville Designs
Center Village, PO Box 806
Harrisville, NH 03450
603-827-3333
Fax: 603-827-3335
Toll-Free Order Line: 800-338-9415
www.harrisville.com
Yarns for knitting and weaving, looms, and spinning accessories.

Henry's Attic
Natural Fiber Yarns
5 Mercury Avenue
Monroe, NY 10950-5226
845-783-3930
Fax: 845-782-2548
Natural fiber, undyed yarns, and custom yarns.

House of Hemp
Beeston Farm
Marhamchurch
Cornwall EX23 0ET
UK
Fax: 44 (0)1288 381638
www.houseofhemp.co.uk
email: shopping@houseofhemp.co.uk
Natural and plant-dyed hemp yarns.

Interweave Press
201 East Fourth Street
Loveland, CO 80537
Toll Free: 800-272-2193
www.interweave.com
email: CustomerService@interweave.com
*Books and publications on fiber. Excellent source
of detailed information—much of it discussed in
The Natural Knitter.*

Kremer Pigmente
228 Elizabeth Street
New York, NY 10012
212-219-2394
Toll Free: 800-995-5501
www.kremer-
pigmente.de/englisch/homee.htm
email: kremerinc@aol.com
Natural dyes and pigments.

La Lana Wools
136-C Paseo Norte
Taos, NM 87571
505-758-9631
Toll Free: 888-377-9631
www.lalanawools.com
email: lalana@lalanawools.com
*Handspun yarn, millspun yarn, plant dyes,
dyeing services, patterns and kits, and fiber
for spinning.*

Lanaknits
105 Park Street
Nelson, BC V1L 2G5
Toll Free: 888-301-0011
www.lanaknits.com
Hemp yarn.

Lorna's Laces
4229 North Honore Street
Chicago, IL 60613
773-935-3803
www.lornaslaces.net
email: yarn@lornaslaces.net
Hand-dyed yarn.

Louet
RR 4
Prescott Ontario, K0E 1T0
613-925-4502
www.louet.com
email: info@louet.com
*Yarns, dyes, fibers, patterns, and spinning and
weaving equipment.*

Magpie Woodworks
316 Parkwood Drive
Grand Junction, CO 81503
970-256-1257
email: magpiwdwks@aol.com
*Handcrafted wooden needlework equipment,
including etui cases for double-pointed needles
and tapestry needles.*

Mini-Mills
RR#1
Belfast
Prince Edward Island
Canada C0A1A0
Fax: 902-659-2248
Toll Free Order Line: 800-827-3397
www.minimills.net
*A fully operational mill that specializes in hard-
to-find fibers; the store offers many supplies for
weavers and spinners.*

Morehouse Farm
2 Rock City Road
Milan, NY 12571
845-758-3710
Toll Free: 866-470-4852
www.morehousefarm.com
email: MerinoWool@MorehouseFarm.com
*Merino yarn, fleece and roving, kits, patterns,
and accessories.*

Mostly Merino
Margaret Klein Wilson
PO Box 878
Putney VT 05346
802-254-7436
www.mostlymerino.com
email: merino@together.net
*Hand-dyed luxury merino/mohair blend knitting
yarns in a distinctive color palette.*

Mountain Colors
PO Box 156
Corvallis, MT 59828
406-777-2277
www.mountaincolors.com
Handpainted and hand-dyed yarns.

Mountain Shadow Farms
Chris Lyczynski & Leigh Chandler
60 Orr Road
Jericho, VT 05465
802-899-5164
www.mountainshadowfarm.com
email: thellama@mountainshadowfarm.com
*Handspun, hand-dyed, and handknit clothing
and accessories. Exotic fibers, including qiviut,
guanaco, yak, cashmere, and mulberry silk.*

Muench
1323 Scott Street
Petaluma, CA 94954-1135
707-763-9377
Toll Free: 800-733-9276
www.muenchyarns.com
email: info@muenchyarns.com
Yarns, patterns, and accessories.

Oomingmak
Alaskan Musk Ox Producers's Cooperative
604 H Street
Anchorage, AK
907-272-9225
Toll Free: 888-360-9665
www.qiviut.com
email: qiviut@gci.net
Qiviut fiber, yarn, and finished goods.

Peace Fleece
475 Porterfield Road
Porter, ME 04068
www.peacefleece.com
email: saw@peacefleece.com
*Yarns, patterns, kits, and accessories. Fleece and
roving. Finished goods.*

Peace of Yarn
626 East Kilbourn Avenue, #1808
Milwaukee, WI 53202
310-497-8031
www.peaceofyarn.com
email: info@peaceofyarn.com
*Exotic fibers for spinning, including guanaco,
vicuna, cashmere, silk, angora, alpaca, llama,
camel, yak, merino, and corriedale.*

Philosopher's Wool
2 Alma Street
Inverhuron, Ontario N0G2T0
519-368-5354
www.philosopherswool.com
email: philosophers88@magma.ca
All-natural wool yarn.

Snow Star Farms
Lovern Mill Road
Antrim, NH 03440
603-588-2552
email: snowstar@tds.net
Corriedale and romney wool yarns, dyed tagua nut buttons.

Thirteen Mile Farm Lamb & Wool Company
13000 Springhill Road
Belgrade, MT 59714
406-388-4945
www.lambandwool.com
email: becky@lambandwool.com
Yarn, fleece for spinning, and finished goods.

Turn of Century
1676 Millsboro Road
Mansfield, OH 44906-3374
419-529-8876
www.turn-of-the-century.com
email: bill@turn-of-the-century.com
Handcrafted wooden knitting needles, crochet hooks, and tatting shuttles.

Vreseis Limited
PO Box 69
Guinda, CA 95637
530-796-3007
info@vreseis.com
www.vreseis.com
Organic, naturally colored cotton fiber for spinning, weaving, and knitting.

Windy Valley Muskox
HC 04 Box 9220
Palmer, AK 99645
907-745-1005
www.windyvalleymuskox.com
email: info@windyvalleymuskox.com
Qiviut, suri alpaca, cashmere, and Peruvian cotton yarn.

Woodland Woolworks
100 East Washington Street
PO Box 850
Carlton, OR 97111
800-547-3725
www.woodlandwoolworks.com
Supplies for handspinners, weavers, and knitters

offering a wide selection of spinning fibers, exotic fibers, spinning wheels, drum carders, books, weaving looms, knitting needles, yarns, and gadgets.

The Wool Room
172 Joe's Hill Road
Brewster, NY 10509
845-279-7627, by appointment only
www.woolroom.com
email: susan@woolroom.com
Spinning wheels, looms (from rigid heddle to 32-harness computer assisted), David Reed Smith spindles, and other wooden accessories and fiber.

Wooly Warren
1440 Quinalt Street
Springfield, OR 97477
541-746-5820
email: woolywarren@yahoo.com
Exotic spinning supplies, commission handspun yarns, buffalo fiber, and yarn.

Yarns International
PO Box 467
Cabin John, MD 20818
301-229-4203
Toll Free: 800-927-6728 (orders only)
www.yarnsinternational.com
email: info@yarnsinternational.com
Natural colored Shetland wool yarns.

ORGANIZATIONS

Alpaca Owners and Breeders of America
5000 Linbar Drive, Suite 297
Nashville, TN 37211
615-834-4195
email: info@aobamail.com
www.alpacaowners.com

Colored Angora Goat Breeders Association
www.cagba.org
email: info@cagba.org
email: CAGBA_stan@ferncrestfarm.com

Organic Trade Association, The
PO Box 547
Greenfield, MA 01302
413-774-7511
www.ota.com

Pygora Goat Breeders Association
538 Lamson Road
Lysander, NY 13027
315-678-2812
www.pygoragoats.org
email: pbaregistrar@aol.com

CONTRIBUTORS

PHOTOGRAPHY
Alexandra Grablewski

Alexandra is a photographer based in New York City. Whether traveling or working in her Lower East Side studio, she enjoys shooting a combination of food, still-life, and lifestyle subjects. In addition to having photographed several cooking and craft books, her work can be seen in such magazines as *Martha Stewart Living* and *Real Simple*.

TECHNICAL EDITOR
AND DESIGNER
Charlotte Quiggle

Born and raised in Minnesota, Charlotte ventured to Yale College where she majored in French literature. After working at *TIME* magazine for 16 years, Charlotte decided to become a Certified Financial Planner and began doing tax work.

During all this time, Charlotte's fingers were working her needles fast and furiously as an antidote to the stresses of Manhattan's professional life. When she was no longer required to work 80 hours a week at *TIME*, Charlotte joined the Big Apple Knitters Guild (BAKG) and later became its program chair. She also served on the organizing committee for the first New York City Knit Outs.

Eventually, Charlotte found tax work taxing and began publishing designs in *Interweave Knits*, *Knitters*, *Knit It!*, *Vogue Knitting*, and *Knit 1*. In addition to *The Natural Knitter*, she was also the technical editor for *The Green Mountain Spinnery Knitting Book*, *Cables Untangled*, and the magazines *Knit It!* and *Cast On*, as well as for yarn companies.
PROJECT: Arthur's Field of Dreams Sweater (page 74)

PROJECT SHEPHERDESS
Lynn Albright

The Project Shepherdess of *The Natural Knitter* comes to the world of knitting and fiber through her older sister, Barbara, the book's author. Barb, the ultimate Big Sister, introduced Lynn to knitting when she was eight-years-old. Decades later, Lynn found herself advancing these early skills when asked to design a few projects for some of Barb's books.

A marketer by trade, Lynn's professional skills were valuable in helping to organize and "shepherd" the varying elements of this book through completion. During this immersion, she has discovered a new-found appreciation for natural fibers. As the final pieces of this book were coming together, Lynn found herself the proud owner of three sheep fleeces, which she is in the process of washing. From there she plans to card the wool, spin it, dye it (with plant dyes), and knit it, so that she can truly be a "natural knitter."

DESIGNERS
Beth Brown-Reinsel

Beth Brown-Reinsel has been involved in many facets of the fiber arts as a spinner, basket weaver, dyer, knitter, former yarn shop and mail-order business owner, author, and knitwear designer—but teaching is her passion. She has worked in production, as well as in creating and teaching courses and workshops, both locally and nationally. She developed and implemented the correspondence course, "Traditional Ganseys" for The Knitting Guild of America for 11 years. Beth also authored the book *Knitting Ganseys*, published by Interweave Press. Her articles have appeared in *Threads*, *Cast On*, *Interweave Knits*, and *Knitter's* magazines. She continues to design for yarn companies, magazines, and her own pattern line.
PROJECT: Ålvros Sweater (page 40)

Carol Cypher

A professional fiber artist, Carol focuses on feltmaking and beadwork, and the provocative pairing of the two. A very busy and popular teacher, she takes a fresh and contemporary approach to teaching these ancient crafts at national conferences, craft schools, art schools, guilds, cultural centers, and galleries. Her wearable art and designs are published in magazines and books and shown in galleries in New York, Connecticut, and New Jersey. Everything related to fiber interests Carol and she also spins, knits, crochets, and recently has enjoyed working with a lucet. Check out carolcypher.com.
PROJECT: The Felted Bead Diva's Flowers (page 178)

Judy Dercum

Judy Dercum is a knitwear designer and teacher who specializes in using color. She is best known for her numerous intarsia designs influenced by the landscape and colors of the American Southwest. Her work has appeared in several books, including: *Knitting in America, Knitter's Stash, Handpaint Country, Simple Knits for Sophisticated Living,* and *Knitting Made Easy,* as well as in the magazines *Knits, Knitter's,* and *InKnitters.* A former Olympic-class skier, Judy knows her way around the great outdoors.

PROJECT: Taos Saltillo Jacket (page 158)

Valentina Devine

Born in Moscow and raised in Berlin, Valentina moved to the U.S. in the 1950s and reports that she has always been a knitter. She says, "I can remember knitting all sorts of things from doll clothes to small garments for myself. During the war years we had to use the most unusual materials, from the cotton strings of a mop to cut-up nylon stockings. To this day I enjoy knitting with any kind of material I can get on my knitting needle."

In the beginning, Valentina knitted mostly monochromatic garments, always following (and agonizing over) a pattern. In the 70s, she began to "paint with yarn," her style changing to free form and abstract shapes and color combinations.

A contributor to many knitting books and publications, Valentina has also taught the technique of "Creative Knitting" for 22 years. She now resides in Los Alamos, New Mexico.

PROJECT: Chenille in the Morning (page 124)

Norah Gaughan

Norah confesses that she was born into a family of fiber snobs and that her early knitting teachers taught her using pure wool and alpaca. She has overcome some of that bias, but she still finds her greatest joy is in working with natural fibers.

A very prolific designer, her first design was published during high school. After graduating from Brown University, she freelanced in the hand-knitting industry and, for a while, specialized in stitch development, selling her designs to Seventh Avenue and major textile manufacturing companies. Her next move was to be design director at JCA Inc., the parent company of Reynolds, Adrienne Vittadini Yarns, and Artful Yarns. Now, Norah is back in the freelance world, exploring her own route in the design process.

PROJECT: Architectural Rib Pullover (page 86)

Darlene Hayes

Darlene is the owner and creative brain behind Hand Jive Knits (handjiveknits.com), a small company specializing in naturally dyed yarns and fibers and patterns for handknitters. This is her third career, after working as a research molecular biologist and an attorney. She keeps her legal mind sharp by continuing to research and write about legal issues that impact the fiber arts and the people who practice them.

Her enduring interest in knitting led her to begin publishing her own knitting patterns, which in turn led to dyeing a line of yarn that matched her design vision. In addition to her self-published line and designs for major yarn companies, her work can be seen in books and magazines including *Knitter's, INKnitters, Cast On, Ultimate Knitting, Simple Knits for Sophisticated Living, Vogue Knitting, Baby Knits Two,* and *Odd Ball Knitting.*

PROJECT: It's a Mod, Mod Modular Hat, Socks, and Half-Gloves (page 152)

Lidia Karabinich

Lidia moved to New York in 1993 after studying and teaching chemistry for 10 years in eastern Ukraine, her homeland. She worked for several years in a retail yarn shop doing custom knitting patterns and teaching machine knitting. Later, Lidia established her own company, LNK Knitwear, producing samples for Seventh Avenue design houses and SoHo boutiques. A frequent designer for yarn companies and for publications such as *Interweave Knits* and *Vogue Knitting,* Lidia is now the store designer for String, a yarn boutique on Madison Avenue in New York.

PROJECT: Memories of Ukraine (page 130)

Jennifer Lindsay

Jennifer Lindsay is a lifelong knitter and published designer who is "passionate about every aspect of the craft—from fibers and colors to history, techniques, and design." Jennifer works part time at Yarns International in Bethesda, Maryland, where she also teaches private knitting lessons. In addition, she is a co-founder with Laurie Gonyea of Destination Knits—a business designed to provide knitting workshops to knitters of all abilities in a relaxing and rejuvenating setting. Jennifer lives in Chevy Chase, Maryland, with her husband Wade and their two dogs, Tempest and Keeper.

PROJECTS: Shetland Fern (page 34) and Lucky Fish Mini Case (page 170)

Sheila Meyer

As a "lefty," no one wanted to teach Sheila to knit, so she bought some books and taught herself! Sheila soon found herself a fixture at the local yarn shop and was offered a job. After managing several yarn stores, she took her fascination with the structure of stitches on to freelance for such leading designers as Perry Ellis, Ralph Lauren, Calvin Klein, Donna Karan, and the Gap.

Knitting has taken Sheila around the world, working with worldwide organizations and NGOs, and starting knitting workshops and cooperatives in Peru, Armenia, Croatia, and other countries. During her travels, she discovered a new fascination—the buttons of the world! Sheila now finds herself the busy owner of One World Button Supply Co.

PROJECT: Bodacious Bunny Baby Set (page 104)

Marjorie Moureau

Marjorie, who trained at Le Cordon Bleu and worked in test kitchens, has loved to knit and crochet throughout all the chapters of her life. In addition to teaching at The Vermont Yarn Company in Middlebury, Vermont, Marj has since learned to handspin and dye, and runs a weekly afterschool knitting group at her local elementary school. In the works are a series of her simple patterns for "distracted knitters."

PROJECT: Back Home in Vermont Sweater (page 48)

Debbie New

Born and raised in Australia, where she learned to knit as a very small girl, Debbie has lived in several countries, settling finally in Canada. She is the mother of eight and grandmother of many and has enjoyed a number of interrupted careers: microbiologist, teacher, symphony violinist, potter, and biomedical engineer.

Her unusual knitting patterns and artworks have appeared in knitting magazines, in books such as *A Gathering of Lace*, *For the Love of Knitting*, *Socks, Socks, Socks*, and her own book, *Unexpected Knitting*, as well as in art galleries, textile museums, and, individually, in juried shows. She has given talks and workshops around the world. Her regional Arts Council chose her as the Visual Artist of the year in 1997.

In the summer, Debbie lives on a narrow boat barge in England. Her Cast Off Sweater was designed one summer between working the locks.

PROJECT: Cast Off Sweater (page 136)

Linda Romens

Linda—a native of Madison, Wisconsin, who now makes her home in Taos, New Mexico—has always found herself drawn to natural fibers and jumped at the chance to design and knit a garment made of qiviut— often prohibitively expensive—for *The Natural Knitter*. In addition to spinning her brothers' llama's wool, Linda also spins her dog's fur to use in knitting projects!

In addition to spinning her own yarn and designing knitting patterns, Linda is a glass artist, working in both stained glass and fusing dichroic glass pieces in a kiln, and silversmith. Her "real job" is in medical technology, where she works in the laboratory at Holy Cross Hospital in Taos.

PROJECT: Qiviut Twinset (page 94)

Janet Scanlon

Janet Scanlon lives and works on a cranberry farm on Oregon's Pacific Coast. She says, "It's a lifestyle that gives me time to think and create." Janet's mother taught her to knit 40 years ago, and yarn and needles are her constant companions. Their portability gives her the chance to enjoy them everywhere, even while tending cranberries.

"I love fiber—dyeing it, spinning it, weaving it, crocheting it, knitting it. Everything about yarn and fiber is a pleasure to me. I've never met a yarn shop I didn't like."

Including her own! For several years, Janet was a partner at Coos Bay's My Yarn Shop and has built a thriving Internet business selling patterns at her website, knitkit.com. Janet lives on Cape Blanco in Oregon with Roy, Isaac, and Inky.

PROJECT: Little Sit-sters (page 16) and Daydream: Knitter's Meditation Mat & Bag (page 28)

Vicki Square

Vicki Square is passionate about her creative pursuits in the fiber arts. She designs knitted pieces from elegant basics to unique art to wear. Her strengths in color and texture are stated boldly through her engineering of unusually shaped garments and accessories. Vicki is the author of the popular *Knitter's Companion*, *Folk Bags*, *Folk Hats*, and *Knit Great Basics*. Magazines have featured her work, and she has won awards for her innovative designs. She regularly teaches workshops locally, regionally, and throughout the country. She earned her MFA in printmaking at Colorado State University in Fort Collins, Colorado, where she lives with her family.

PROJECT: The Uma Sweater (page 112)

Setsuko Torii

Based in Kyoto, Japan, Setsuko studied knitwear design at the Ichida Knitting School. While there, she met her business partner, Masami Fukui. Setsuko works with Masami's yarns, sometimes as single strands and sometimes in combination, to create garments that have a minimalist structure. Their yarns and distinctive line of knitwear is carried by Habu, a New York weaving studio and showroom where they occasionally teach courses.

PROJECT: Pineapple Overtop (page 142)

Margaret Klein Wilson

Margaret Klein Wilson is the owner of Mostly Merino, a fiber studio specializing in hand-dyed luxury merino and mohair knitting yarns, patterns, and knitting kits since 1990. Mostly Merino was born after Margaret, having relocated her family from Boston to southern Vermont, found herself the shepherdess to a few Merino sheep. A self-taught shepherd, dyer, and designer, Margaret finds her inspiration as much in the process and collaborative nature of bringing wool to market, as she does in the satisfaction of keeping sheep.

Margaret is the author and editor of *The Green Mountain Spinnery Knitting Book*. Her writing and patterns have appeared in *Interweave Knits*, *Handwoven*, and *Knit Lit: I, II, & III*.

PROJECT: Here & There—Stone's Sweater (page 54)

Anna Zilboorg

Anna is an Anglican solitary in the Blue Ridge Mountains. She has pursued knitting styles and patterns around the world. Her marvelous knitting books cover the extremities—*Fancy Feet*, *Fine and Fanciful Hats*, and *Magnificent Mittens*—but one of her books, *Knitting for Anarchists*, takes an analytical look at the whole craft. Most recently, she has published a second edition of *Socks for Sandals and Clogs*. In the past, she has reared children, taught literature and writing at the Massachusetts Institute of Technology, made quilts in Appalachia, and served as a housemother for homeless young men in New York. At present, she comes out of the hermitage only to teach.

PROJECT: Think Zinnias! (page 164)

Kathy Zimmerman

An incredibly talented and prolific designer, Kathy designs from one to three sweaters a month. One to two dozen of her patterns are published in the knitting magazines and in yarn company collections each year. She reports that she does have some help with the actual knitting and that her husband Tim takes care of the mail orders, website, and the homefront (including the cooking). She is also the owner of a knitting store, Kathy's Kreations, in scenic Ligonier, Pennsylvania. The shop started as a custom hand-knitting business, but soon Kathy started stocking the items she needed for her own knitting!

PROJECT: Girls' Night Out Sweater and Hat (page 66)

INDEX